Will jellyfish rule the world?

Leo Hickman is a weekly columnist for the *Guardian*.
His hands-on approach to green living is honest and inspiring.
He has written several books for adults including the bestselling
A Life Stripped Bare: My Year Trying to Live Ethically and
A Good Life: *The Guide to Living Ethically*.

Will jellyfish rule the world?

a book about climate change

LEO HICKMAN

PUFFIN

For Esme, Jessie and Jacob

PUFFIN BOOKS

Published by the Penguin Group
Penguin Books Ltd, 80 Strand, London WC2R 0RL, England
Penguin Group (USA) Inc., 375 Hudson Street, New York, New York 10014, USA
Penguin Group (Canada), 90 Eglinton Avenue East, Suite 700,
Toronto, Ontario, Canada M4P 2Y3 (a division of Pearson Penguin Canada Inc.)
Penguin Ireland, 25 St Stephen's Green, Dublin 2, Ireland (a division of Penguin Books Ltd)
Penguin Group (Australia), 250 Camberwell Road, Camberwell, Victoria 3124, Australia
(a division of Pearson Australia Group Pty Ltd)
Penguin Books India Pvt Ltd, 11 Community Centre, Panchsheel Park,
New Delhi – 110 017, India
Penguin Group (NZ), 67 Apollo Drive, Rosedale, North Shore 0632, New Zealand
(a division of Pearson New Zealand Ltd)
Penguin Books (South Africa) (Pty) Ltd, 24 Sturdee Avenue, Rosebank,
Johannesburg 2196, South Africa

Penguin Books Ltd, Registered Offices: 80 Strand, London WC2R 0RL, England

puffinbooks.com

First published 2009
1

Text copyright © Leo Hickman, 2009
Illustrations copyright © Sara Flavell, 2009
Graph p.84 copyright © *Climate Change 2001: The Scientific Basis*. Contribution of Working
Group I to the Third Assessment Report of the Intergovernmental Panel on Climate Change.
Figure 1. Cambridge University Press.
Photographs p.109 copyright © Archivo Museo Salesiano; copyright © 2004 – Greenpeace/Beltra

Every effort has been made to trace the copyright holders.
The publishers would like to hear from any copyright or source holder not acknowledged.

The moral right of the author and illustrator has been asserted

The website links in this book are to third-party Internet websites which are controlled
and maintained by others. These links are included solely for the convenience of readers
and do not constitute any endorsement by Penguin Books Limited ('Penguin') of the sites linked
or referred to, nor does Penguin have any control over or responsibility for the
content of any such sites.

Set in Formata, Jacoby and Squarehouse by Perfect Bound Ltd
Made and printed in England by Clays Ltd, St Ives plc

British Library Cataloguing in Publication Data
A CIP catalogue record for this book is available from the British Library

ISBN: 978-0-141-32334-3

www.greenpenguin.co.uk

CONTENTS

4   THE EFFECTS OF CLIMATE CHANGE 107

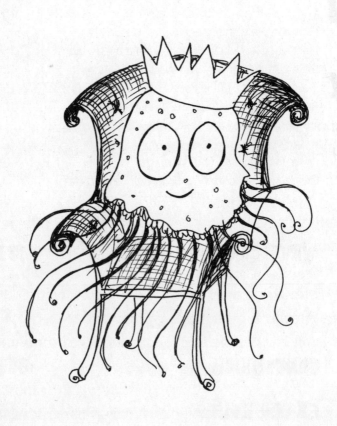

INTRODUCTION

A re jellyfish *really* going to rule the world? Perhaps the better question to think about is: *why* would it ever be likely that jellyfish end up ruling the world? And the answer to that question is the subject of this book: climate change.

Climate change has become the most important issue of our age – perhaps of all human history – because it affects every single person on this planet.

For the first time in our planet's history just one species – human beings: you and me – is causing the climate to change. And if we continue to pollute our environment, we will see more and more disastrous events: flooding, hurricanes, heatwaves, animal extinctions, failed harvests and so on.

But! There **really** are lots of things that you,

your friends and family can do that will make a difference. In this book you will discover what the climate actually is, as well as how and why it's changing, but most importantly you will learn how together we can help minimize the impact of climate change.

So, come on – if you want to prevent a future in which jellyfish might end up ruling the world (for full scary details turn to page 118), then sit down, make yourself comfortable and start reading this book!

OUR PLANET

This planet we call home is very special. In fact, when you look at the long history of Earth, it's remarkable that there's any life to be found here at all, let alone so-called 'advanced' life-forms such as ourselves. Our planet's seen it all: fires, ice, poisonous gases and huge volcanic eruptions. But it's now, at this precise moment in time, that all the elements are just right to produce the perfect conditions for life – from the very highest mountains to the depths of the deepest seas, life can be found . . .

The ONE-MINUTE history of Planet Earth

Humans haven't been on this planet for long. And in terms of the looooong history of Planet Earth, we will only be a mere sentence. In fact, if you imagine the lifespan of Earth as the 12 hours of a clock, with each hour representing one billion years, we are currently only at **half past four**. The entire period in which advanced animal and plant life-forms (which, for a comparatively short time, will include humans) are expected to be on Earth represents just one hour – and we are already about 30 minutes into that hour. By **8 o'clock**, scientists believe, the sun will have expanded and heated up so much that all our oceans will have evaporated into space. And at **12 o'clock** – in 7.5 billion years' time – the Earth will end, engulfed by the sun which itself will be in its death-throes. Therefore, not only is Planet Earth a special place, but we are alive during a very, very special time during its lifespan.

HOW LONG HAVE WE BEEN HERE?

If the lifetime of the Earth was compressed into a single hour, then mankind has been here for . . . **0.157 seconds**.

Turn to page 206 for a timeline of life on Earth . . .

Why is Planet Earth so special?

It's **unique**! We know of no other place like it anywhere else in the universe. Most importantly, the one thing that makes it so special to us is that it is home to life. We have looked long and hard out into space – the moon, Mars and beyond – but, so far, we haven't found any other life out there. We're like a paradise island in the middle of a vast ocean. It's a lonely, but lucky, place to be.

And, of course, it's our **home**. It's all we've got – until, that is, we start building space colonies, but that's a few years off and it's probably best to get the hang of looking after this home first before we make such plans. Like anything that's precious to us, we need to work hard to protect it.

THE GOLDILOCKS PLANET

Many different ingredients have come together for a brief period of time to produce exactly the right conditions to create the world we see today, and a big one of these is **temperature**. Remember how Goldilocks preferred porridge that wasn't too hot or too cold, but just right? Well, Planet Earth is just the right distance from the sun to allow life to thrive. Any closer and it would be too hot, any further away and it would be too cold. We can look at the different average temperatures on Venus, Earth and Mars to see just how lucky we are to have such a hospitable one. Venus is closer to the sun than Earth, and its surface temperature is 460°C – about twice as hot as the oven in your kitchen gets. Meanwhile, on Mars, which is further away from the sun than Earth, the average temperature is −46°C – about as warm as it ever gets on the South Pole during winter. Here on Earth, the average temperature is 14°C – just right for life.

THE GIANT BLANKET

Another vital ingredient for life is the Earth's **atmosphere** – the layer of gases that wrap around the surface of the planet. The Earth's gravity makes sure these gases – which we call 'air' – don't disappear into space. (Gravity is a special force that behaves a bit like when a magnet 'pulls' a metal such as iron towards it.) This is a big relief because without the atmosphere there would be no life on Earth. Just look at the moon: it doesn't have an atmosphere and therefore is freezing cold and has no water, and when was the last time you saw anything living there?

The Earth is very different from the moon, thankfully; our atmosphere acts like a giant blanket, keeping the surface of the planet much, much warmer than it would be if it wasn't there. This process is the Greenhouse

AMAZING FACTS! Air is ... HEAVY!

Ever wondered how heavy all that air is above us all? No? Well, I'll tell you anyway. About 5 quadrillion tonnes. That's 5,000,000,000,000,000 tonnes. Or, put another way, the equivalent to 345 trillion double-decker buses. (That's without any passengers inside, mind you.)

WILL JELLYFISH RULE THE WORLD?

Effect and plays a very important role in understanding how our climate acts – and the problems our climate now faces.

The atmosphere – and, therefore, the air we breathe – is made up of lots of different gases, but the most important are nitrogen (78 per cent), oxygen (21 per cent), argon (1 per cent) and carbon dioxide. Carbon dioxide makes up only about 0.38 per cent of the air we breathe, but this amount is rising each year as we put more and more carbon dioxide into the air by burning fossil fuels, such as oil and coal. Scientists now say that this extra carbon dioxide, in addition to some

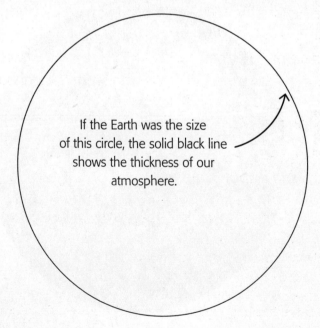

If the Earth was the size of this circle, the solid black line shows the thickness of our atmosphere.

other polluting gases, is causing the average global temperature to rise, which in turn is likely to cause some big changes to our climate over the coming decades.

SPLISH SPLASH

We live in a wonderful, but delicately balanced, world. Our atmosphere is keeping us both snug and supplied with fresh air to breathe. But the one thing that really sets our planet apart from others that also orbit the sun is the presence of liquid **water** – and lots of it. If you could gather up all the Earth's water together into a giant sphere, it would amount to 1,360 million cubic

All the Earth's water gathered into a sphere

WILL JELLYFISH RULE THE WORLD?

kilometres in volume, measuring 1,400km across at its diameter – the same as the distance from London to Rome.

Just over two-thirds of the Earth's surface is covered in sea water. Our oceans and seas are home to a rich variety of life, but this mass of water is also vital to life on the land, too. Without the evaporation of sea water, there would be no rain or snow – part of a wider process called the **water cycle**. Without this precipitation there would be no fresh water, so land-based animals – such as humans – wouldn't survive very long at all. Fresh water is a pretty rare commodity on Earth – it actually

AMAZING FACTS! Swim every mountain

Everyone knows that the world's tallest mountain is Mount Everest in the Himalayas, right? Measuring from sea-level to the tip of its summit, it stands 8,848 metres high. But it is not actually the tallest mountain in the world. That honour goes to a sea mountain called Mauna Kea in Hawaii. Measuring from the base of the mountain situated on the sea floor to its peak (which stands 4,205 metres above sea-level), Mauna Kea is 10,314 metres tall – almost 1.5 kilometres taller than Mount Everest!

makes up a tiny percentage of the entire mass of water on the planet. Just 2 per cent, in fact.

Our oceans are so vast that much of what lies under the surface is virtually unexplored by humans. Some scientists think we know more about the surface of the moon or Mars than we know about the bottom of our oceans. The Mariana Trench in the Western Pacific, the deepest anywhere in the world, is almost 11,000 metres deep at its deepest point (that's equivalent to 34 Eiffel Towers stacked on top of each other!). But even though some strange creatures lurk at the bottom of the oceans – just take a look at the super-ugly angler fish with its sharp buck-teeth – most of the life in our oceans lives comparatively close to the surface where the sun's light and warming rays can still be found. However, the world's oceans and seas offer a variety of very different homes to life, ranging from the coral reefs in the tropics through to the freezing waters of the polar regions.

THE DRY BITS

But not all the Earth's surface is covered in water. There are the dry bits, of course, where we live. Even so, water still plays a hugely important role on land, too. There are hundreds of different types of habitat on land, from mountain ranges and tropical jungles to coastal marshes and deserts. The conservation charity WWF says that there are 13 distinct land-based **biomes** – basic types of habitat – on Earth, distinguished by their differing climates and geographical features. These range from the tundra of Siberia and temperate broadleaf forests of Britain, through to the deserts found in places like Chile and Arizona and mangrove swamps of the tropics. (The WWF says there are also 12 sea-based biomes ranging from the ice-cold seas of Antarctica through to the warm tropical corals.)

Land is ever-changing too, though you probably won't notice, as it can take millions of years to occur. Mountain ranges rise and fall, coastlines are washed away by waves, and new land climbs out of the sea. This is partly due to the movement and erosion of water. Only a few thousand years ago, you could have walked from London to Paris without getting wet. There used to be a land bridge between England and France, but then the sea level rose and the land bridge was flooded, forming the English Channel.

Changes like these have been occurring ever since the Earth was first formed more than four billion years ago. Some scientists believe that in 250 million years' time, all the world's continents will have collided together again and formed a supercontinent like the one called Pangea that existed 250 million years ago.

Mother Earth

Many cultures around the world call our planet 'Mother Earth'. It's one way of recognizing that our planet's most remarkable distinguishing factor is, of course, the life that it supports and nurtures. And we're not talking about a humble microbe that may or may not be lurking under a stone on, say, Mars. The vast variety of advanced life on Earth must make it one of the most amazing places anywhere in the universe. While we don't yet know if life exists elsewhere in the universe, chances are it does, given how unfathomably vast the universe is. Surely Earth isn't a one-off fluke? What we do know is that we still haven't located life, and we have been looking hard with space probes and telescopes across millions of kilometres out into space. If advanced life-forms, as seen on Earth, do exist elsewhere then they are a very long way away – and they haven't made contact with us yet, or not that we know of!

UP ABOVE AND DOWN BELOW

Without our atmosphere, life wouldn't exist on Earth. But it is not the only home to life on Earth. At the very bottom of our deep oceans and in the very deepest caves, life has been found, too. The entire region of the Earth where life has been found is known as

the **biosphere**. Its extent is still being determined by scientists, but we know that birds do not fly any higher than about 12,000 metres. Rüppell's vultures, a breed of bird that lives in central Africa, have been spotted flying at an altitude of about 6,000 metres – but an aeroplane flying at 11,300 metres once collided with one of these creatures, proving that they can fly much higher if they wish! Meanwhile, mysterious life-forms have been found as deep down as 11,000 metres beneath the water's surface in some of the world's deepest sea trenches. At the very bottom of the Mariana Trench scientists using special submarines (the water pressure down there is like having 50 jumbo jets sitting on your head!) have found tiny single-celled organisms called foraminifera, which belong to a kingdom of life-forms known as protists, including algae and slime moulds.

These extremes may seem remarkable to us, but they show that the extent of life on Earth only extends to a 23km-thick band on the surface of the planet. If you think that the diameter of the Earth at the equator is 12,756km, then you can see just how thin the biosphere is compared to the width of the planet. When viewed from space,

Critical mass

If you were to weigh all the world's life, which type of life do you think would tip the scales? Animals, perhaps? Think how much all those whales, elephants, humans, cows, etc. would weigh together. Or what about plants? All those trees must weigh a tremendous amount. Actually, the correct answer is that the world's micro-organisms account for about 60 per cent of the entire mass of Planet Earth's life.

WILL JELLYFISH RULE THE WORLD?

astronauts have remarked how vulnerable and small the biosphere actually appears compared against the size of the Earth.

THAT'S LIFE

Having already had a few billion years to evolve and develop, life on this planet is extremely diverse and complex. There are four main types of life on Earth – plants, animals, fungi and micro-organisms. Even though we have been studying and searching for new species on Earth for centuries, we are still making new discoveries all the time, particularly in life-rich environments such as rainforests. In fact, about half of the world's plant and animal species are believed to be found within its rainforests, which account for just 7 per cent of its landmass. The Amazon rainforest in South America, which is the world's largest, is home to about 2.5 million insect species, tens of thousands of plants and at least 2,000 species of birds and mammals. They're the ones we know about, anyway.

In total, across the whole planet, about 1.7 million plant and animal species have so far been identified by scientists. No one knows for sure how many have yet to be found and recorded, but the best guesses by scientists seem to suggest that there are 15–30 million species in total. Some groups have been exhaustively researched. Scientists believe there are 9,000–10,000 bird species on the planet and don't expect to find too many more. Similarly, there are about 5,400 known mammals, yet discoveries of new mammals are also very rare nowadays. But a lot of mystery and guesswork still surrounds some other animal types. For example, there are probably many millions of insect species out there that have yet to be seen, let alone documented by scientists. Creepy-crawlies are very good at hiding in dark corners!

NOW YOU SEE IT, NOW YOU DON'T

Life is abundant on Earth. This is clear. But just as this planet has experienced mass extinction events in its past, there is a growing fear that, largely due to the actions of just one species – us humans – thousands, if not millions, of species could now be lost forever. In fact, scientists have named it the **Holocene Extinction Event** – the so-called 'Sixth Mass Extinction' on Earth – which reflects the fact that it is occurring during the Holocene, the geological period that began 10,000 years ago at the peak of the last ice age and that has been dominated by the actions of modern mankind.

Scientists fear that up to 140,000 species are being lost every year at present, as humans encroach on or even destroy habitats through farming, fishing, pollution and construction. The rate of extinction is ever accelerating – over the past century up to two million species of animals and plants have been lost.

Compared to the 'normal' rate of extinction dictated by the ordinary evolutionary processes on the planet, today the rate of extinction is running at 100–1,000 times that pace. Many of these species extinctions go unnoticed by most of us as they tend to be creatures such as insects or amphibians that remain out of sight, living deep within a rainforest, but some endangered species do catch our attention, such as polar bears.

Perhaps the most famous extinction of all time was the dodo, a large flightless bird that once lived on the island of Mauritius in the Indian Ocean. It was hunted by early settlers and its habitat was also destroyed. By the late 17th century it was extinct and the animal has since become synonymous with extinction through the use of the phrases 'As dead as a dodo' or 'To go the way of the dodo'. It's now our job to work as hard as we can to make sure no more species go the way of the dodo – including our own.

2

OUR CLIMATE

On a whistle-stop tour of Earth, you would discover wildly diverse worlds – fiery deserts, freezing tundra, lush rainforests and windswept mountains. The sun, snow, rain and wind all shape our landscape – you only need to look out of the window to see this happening. The climate is constantly changing, and has done so for millions of years, but to understand why climate change has now become such a threat to humans, we have to understand a little bit about how our climate works.

Why does it rain so much in Britain?

I know, I know, it gets annoying after a while. But you could ask a similar question anywhere in the world. Why does it snow so much at the South Pole? Why is it so hot and dry in the Sahara desert? Why is it so warm and wet in the Amazon rainforest?

The Earth isn't a uniform place with exactly the same weather in every location. Far from it – and thank goodness. What a boring place it would be if this were the case!

There are four key factors that help determine a region's climate – these are **latitude**, **ocean currents**, **altitude**, and **mountain ranges**. Together these factors mean that different areas of the planet experience very different climates.

FROM TOP TO BOTTOM

A region's **latitude** means how far north or south of the equator it is. The equator is the imaginary line that runs around the middle of the Earth and divides the planet into the north and south hemispheres. The further away from the equator a place is, the more dramatic

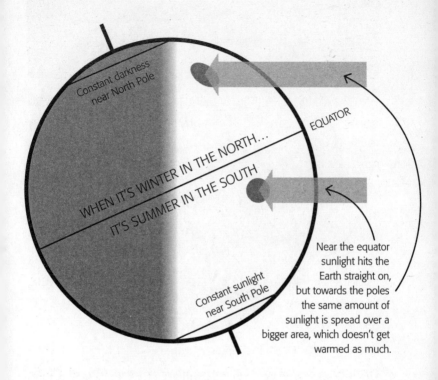

Constant darkness near North Pole

WHEN IT'S WINTER IN THE NORTH...

IT'S SUMMER IN THE SOUTH

EQUATOR

Constant sunlight near South Pole

Near the equator sunlight hits the Earth straight on, but towards the poles the same amount of sunlight is spread over a bigger area, which doesn't get warmed as much.

its seasonal changes will be. This is because the Earth leans slightly (by 23° 26', to be precise) on its axis as it circles the sun. That means at certain times of the year, each hemisphere is either leaning towards or leaning away from the sun. The Earth also moves around the sun, not in a perfect circle, but in an ellipse, which is a slightly squashed-looking circle. Both these factors combine to create our seasons.

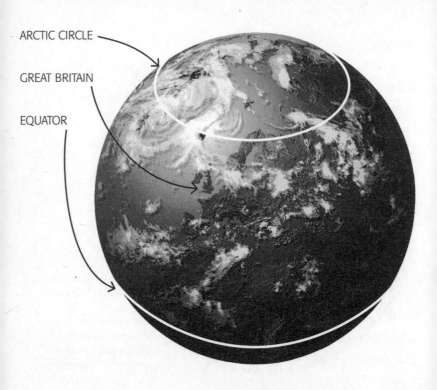

ARCTIC CIRCLE

GREAT BRITAIN

EQUATOR

Britain is roughly halfway between the Arctic Circle and the equator. This means that it has four distinct, roughly equal seasons – spring, summer, autumn and winter. Countries that lie on the equator don't have such distinctive seasons as Britain – in fact, the climate remains relatively constant throughout the year on the equator. In stark contrast, countries close to the poles have very deep winters, with long periods without any daylight. If you travel beyond the Arctic or Antarctic Circles during wintertime, the sun disappears altogether for several months. That's why, for example, male emperor

WILL JELLYFISH RULE THE WORLD?

penguins huddle together in large groups during winter – it's so cold and dark, there's nothing better to do than keep unhatched eggs warm on their feet and wait for the sunlight to return in spring.

But all this only helps to explain why there are big seasonal differences in temperature and sunlight around the world. It still doesn't really explain why it rains so much in Britain.

RIDING THE WAVES

So next we need to look out to sea. **Oceans** play a big part in deciding the type of climate a region experiences. Britain is right next to the Atlantic Ocean, but more significantly it sits at the end of something called the **North Atlantic Drift**. This is the tail-end of an ocean current called the Gulf Stream and it brings warm water from over 6,000km away, all the way from the Caribbean Sea. The prevailing winds, sea surface temperature and saltiness of the sea water all combine to cause this current – and others like it all around the world – to move across the oceans and greatly affect local climatic conditions. The whole network of currents that wrap around the world's oceans like a tangled piece of spaghetti is called the **Great Ocean Conveyor Belt**. And without the North Atlantic Drift, Britain would have a climate similar to Newfoundland in Canada – where temperatures in the winter can fall to as low as −35°C. Now who's complaining about the rain?

DON'T LOOK DOWN

Alongside latitude and ocean currents, the next significant factor that determines climate is **altitude**. Altitude is the height any location is above sea-level. Even though two regions might be at the same latitude as one another, a significant difference in altitude can mean they experience very different climates. This difference is most noticeable in mountain ranges – Mount Kilimanjaro in Tanzania sits very close to the equator and is therefore

Get the drift?

Scientists think that the North Atlantic Drift has been in existence for only about 13,400 years. Without it, northern Europe could slip back into another ice age. There is also some evidence that it moves in a 13–15-year cycle, whereby either it brings more warm waters up to the North Atlantic or, alternatively, it weakens and cooler waters predominate. So the next time someone moans about the weather, remind them what it would be like if we didn't 'catch the drift'.

WILL JELLYFISH RULE THE WORLD?

located within a tropical climate. But snow can be found at the summit of the mountain due to its immense height. This is because the higher you go, the thinner and cooler the air becomes. In fact, for every 300-metre rise in altitude above sea-level, the average temperature drops by 2–3°C.

A PEAK PERFORMER

Mountain ranges also act as a barrier to winds carrying rain. The world's tallest mountain range, the Himalayas, is so vast that it blocks virtually all rain from passing over it. This means that the Indian subcontinent to the south gets deluged with monsoon rains, whereas the Tibetan plateau to the north receives hardly any rain or snow during the year, making it one of the driest places on Earth. Similarly, in Britain, the western fringes of the country, which include the moors and tors of the South-West and the mountains of Wales and Scotland, prevent some of the precipitation carried by the prevailing Atlantic westerly winds from reaching the eastern side of the country. As a result, regions such as the South-East and East Anglia experience less annual rainfall than the western regions.

Mountain ranges also generate winds themselves as air passes up and down their slopes, which, again, can affect local climatic conditions. And well above most mountain ranges lie the jet stream winds. These fast-moving, narrow currents of air move around the planet at speeds of up to 500kmph and altitudes of 10–15km above sea-level. Meteorologists use the position of the jet streams to help them predict the weather. They typically mark the boundary between different climate zones because they are caused by the often extreme temperature differences between two zones.

If the jet stream over the Atlantic pushes further south during the summer months it can bring wet and windy weather thereby ruining what would otherwise be a lovely British summer!

WILL JELLYFISH RULE THE WORLD?

Where are the coldest, hottest, wettest, driest places on Earth?

1 COLDEST: −89.2°C was recorded in Vostok, Antarctica, on 21 July 1983

2 HOTTEST: 58.0°C was recorded in Al Aziziyah, Libya, on 13 September 1922

3 WETTEST: 24,555mm of rain was recorded in Cherrapunjee, north-eastern India, in 1974

4 DRIEST: Virtually no rain has been recorded in the Atacama Desert, northern Chile, over the past century

Which climate would you prefer to live in?

If you could choose just one place to live, would you rather be: on a tropical island, in the middle of a desert, floating on an iceberg, deep in a rainforest, or here in Britain? It's hard to believe sometimes, but Britain has one of the most appealing climates anywhere in the world – it's never too hot and it's never too cold, plus we rarely suffer from extreme droughts. So we're a bit like Planet Earth, really, in that we're a 'Goldilocks' country. We live in what is called a **temperate** climate, which is usually described as a region where average temperatures range between 10°C and above in the summer and –3°C and above in the winter. However, temperate regions also tend to have the most unpredictable weather of any type of climate. But I don't need to tell you that!

Here's what other people around the world have to put up with . . .

TROPICAL

Sounds nice, doesn't it? But that constant heat and humidity could get you down after a while. Tropical regions are found around the equator and have an average temperature of 18°C or higher throughout the entire year. There's also at least 60mm of rainfall to contend with every month. Would you want to live in a place that very rarely, if ever, sees snow?

DRY

Well, how about living in a desert? The Earth's dry regions are among the most inhospitable places of all to live due to the usually searing heat and lack of water. And when it does rain, it tends to come in the form of a storm. Deserts cover roughly a third of the Earth's land surface and even include parts of freezing Antarctica. Don't forget to pack sunglasses and a hat!

POLAR

Think you can handle the cold? Well, you might want to grab a scarf and woolly hat, and zip up your coat, if you plan on living in a place where average temperatures throughout the year remain below 10°C – and often well below that mark. In so-called **tundra** zones, such as Siberia in Russia, average temperatures can stay above 0°C in summer months, but in ice-cap regions such as at the North Pole or in Antarctica average temperatures remain beneath 0°C all year round. At least you wouldn't need to worry about buying a fridge!

What's the difference between climate and weather?

About 30 years. **Weather** is what you see outside your window today. It might be pouring with rain, snowing heavily, or it might be sunny. However, **climate** is the average weather that's been going on outside your window for the past 30 or more years. A weather forecast will vary day to day, but climate can be described in fairly certain terms because it is based on the general weather patterns recorded day by day, month by month, season by season over three or more decades. This is why weather forecasters struggle to tell us with any real accuracy what the weather will be like this time next week, but climatologists (scientists who study the world's climate) can tell us, in general terms, what our climate will be like over the coming seasons and years.

Why did lizards once sunbathe in Antarctica?

Believe it or not, Antarctica was once so warm and humid that it was home to tropical plants and the types of animal species that we would now expect to find near the equator. Instead of seeing penguins huddling up to keep their eggs warm during a freezing winter, as is the case today, Antarctica would have offered the rather odd sight of reptiles, such as lizards, catching a few warming rays in the hot sun, or perhaps taking a dip in the warm coastal waters.

But we are talking 55 million years ago! This was during the Eocene Period, just before Antarctica broke away from the landmass we now know as Australia and drifted south into the cold polar latitudes where it exists today.

In fact, the world's climate has changed, quite dramatically at times, over its long history, and it is still changing today. In fact, it will continue to change until the Earth gets swallowed up by the sun in 7.5 billion years' time.

Just 11,000 years ago, the northern half of Britain was covered in ice two kilometres thick. Imagine trying to make your way to school through that! Today, we are thankfully experiencing a period known as **interglacial** – in other words, we are currently between two ice ages. Make a note in your diary: the next ice age is expected to reach its peak in 80,000 years, but there is still some debate among scientists about when this ice age will begin. Some believe that, based on previous ice age cycles, it could be imminent – perhaps within the next 1,000 years – but that the actions of mankind (as we'll see) might delay its arrival.

The last interglacial period was 130,000 years ago and went on for 10,000–20,000 years. In fact, over the past million years, there have been 10 cycles of spreading then retreating ice sheets. During each ice age, sea levels have dropped dramatically – by up to 120 metres in some cases, which is enough to make much of the North Sea disappear – as the sea water has frozen and become locked up in the ice caps. Up to a third of the planet's land has been covered in vast glaciers during these ice ages, scarring the land's surface with deep valleys as they expand and retreat.

The reason why these ice ages have come in regular cycles over the past few million years is still hotly debated. In truth,

WILL JELLYFISH RULE THE WORLD?

it is likely to be due to a number of different factors, but one of the most popular theories is that tiny wobble-like changes in the Earth's orbit around the sun, and periodic changes in the angle of its tilting axis, help to bring on ice ages every 100,000 years or so. Together these phenomena are known as the **Milankovitch Cycles**.

But just as lizards once sunbathed in Antarctica, so they might do again in the distant future.

Elephants and ice don't go well together. What would happen if the ice broke and the poor elephant fell through into the freezing water below? Given that an elephant can weigh over a tonne, the ice would need to be pretty thick to support it.

Well, believe it or not, in 1814 an elephant was led across the River Thames in London. This was the last time that this river completely froze over from one side to the other. Winters tended to be quite a bit colder then than they are now.

In fact, the northern hemisphere experienced a cooler period – with average temperatures about 1°C lower than today – from the beginning of the 16th century right up to the middle of the 19th century. This 1°C difference was enough to cause significantly deeper, colder winters than we see today. Climatologists have nicknamed this period the **Little Ice Age**.

There is some uncertainty still about how, or why, this period of cooling occurred. Could it have been the unusually high volcanic activity around the world during this period that helped to block out some of the sun's rays?

Or was it the coinciding period of reduced radiation being emitted by the sun? Or even a disruption of the Great Ocean Conveyor Belt?

Some say that the weather in the northern hemisphere changed noticeably following three successive years of torrential rainfall from 1315, which led to widespread crop failures and heralded the Great Famine of 1315–17 that saw millions of people die across Europe. Accounts from that time speak of mass criminality, disease and even cannibalism as law and order collapsed due to the desperate situation the population faced. (And some people think life now is tough!)

But it wasn't until about the 1550s that there was a detectable drop in average temperatures. In Britain, the very worst winter came in 1683/4 and is now known as the **Great Frost**. The River Thames froze solid for two months with ice nearly 30cm thick. There are stories that the sea briefly froze between Dover and Calais, but this now seems a bit unlikely.

The Little Ice Age wasn't a one-off climatic 'hiccup': it followed another climatic blip known as the **Medieval Warming Period**, from 800 to 1300, when it was warm enough throughout much of southern Britain to grow grapes to make wine. This, in turn, followed the **Dark Ages Cold Period**, proving that the climate is ever fluctuating.

So are we now experiencing the next 'warming period' in this long, repeating cycle? Judging by all the evidence we have, it would certainly appear so but, as we will later learn, the big question is whether this is just a natural change, or whether humans are causing (or more likely speeding up) this change through their actions.

'And here's the weather forecast for today ...'

Each morning most of us listen to the weather forecast to help us plan for the day ahead. We need to know whether to grab an umbrella, a thick coat, or wear just a T-shirt. But how would the forecast have sounded during some notable periods in our planet's ever-changing climatic history?

1 JUNE, 3.5 BILLION YEARS BC

'Major news to report today. Liquid water has begun to materialize on the surface of the planet. That's really good news for life. But remember to wear your breathing apparatus when you go outside as the air is thick with carbon dioxide and still remains free of any oxygen. The young sun is still relatively weak and is therefore not offering much in the way of heat, sadly. You might need to wait another billion years or so before we get any decent weather.'

1 JUNE, 55 MILLION YEARS BC

'Hot, hot, hot! Yet another beach day today in Britain, with temperatures soaring into the low 40s. But expect extreme downpours in the afternoon, making for a very humid end to the day. Temperatures at the North Pole today will be a pleasant 24°C, but we're getting reports that the sea there is thick with tropical algae and this is putting off many holidaymakers.'

1 JUNE, 73,000 BC

'The effects of the supervolcanic eruption at Mount Toba in Indonesia are still being felt across the globe today. The average temperature continues to remain at 5°C below the average since the huge explosion cast 1,000 cubic kilometres of rock and ash up into the atmosphere in a 25km-high plume. The human race is now threatened with extinction, with only 10,000 breeding pairs left on the planet. On the bright side, there are signs of a rapid improvement in conditions within the next few years.'

1 JUNE, 15,000 BC

'There are still no signs of the Ice Age relenting. Nothing to report really other than ice, snow, and yet more ice. The English Channel remains a dry, cold valley, while woolly mammoths and woolly rhinoceros roam free across the areas of Europe not covered in thick ice. You might want to put on another jumper.'

1 JUNE, AD 1816

'The "Year Without Summer" continues. The eruption of Mount Tambora in Indonesia during 5–15 April of this year is still causing huge disruption to the weather throughout the world. Crops are failing from Europe through to North America. Food riots have been reported in Britain and in France, as persistent rain and reduced temperatures gravely affect farming.'

1 JUNE, AD 2005

'It's the hottest year on record, according to NASA. They say it hasn't been this hot on the planet for the past 10,000 years. The crown has been snatched from 1998, the previous hottest year on record. This is quite some achievement because the temperatures were driven up in '98 by the last major occurrence of 'El Niño' – a climatic phenomenon that occurs every 3–8 years and sees ocean surface temperatures rise in the Eastern Pacific Ocean around the tropics, which then go on to affect weather conditions across the globe for about 12 months.'

ASTOUNDING SCIENCE!

What is a gas?

On Earth, everything exists in one of three forms: solid, liquid or gas.

Let's use water as an example. When water is frozen it is known as a **solid**. We call it ice, and it's hard and rigid. This is because the tiny, invisible particles inside – called **molecules** – are very tightly bound and locked together.

When the temperature rises, the ice melts and becomes a **liquid**, which we call water. The tiny particles have now loosened up a little and have started to move around, but they are still connected to one another. That's why you can pour a liquid, but you can't pour a solid.

When the temperature gets hot enough – 100°C for water – the liquid water will evaporate into the air and become a **gas**. We call this gas steam. The tiny particles have become so energized by the heat that they can now move around wherever they like and come apart from the rest of the particles. If it isn't contained in a bottle or tank, a gas will mix with the air and become absorbed by the atmosphere. This is why greenhouse gases (see page 51) mix with, and become part of, the atmosphere when they are released.

WILL JELLYFISH RULE THE WORLD?

The Greenhouse Effect – what is it?

If it's freezing cold out in space, why is it warm enough for life not only to survive but to thrive down here on the surface of the Earth? To understand why this happens, and why this warmth doesn't just escape into space, you have to understand a very important process that takes place in our atmosphere called the **Greenhouse Effect**. It is also crucial to understanding why our climate is changing today. You'll be hearing an awful lot about the Greenhouse Effect throughout the rest of your life, so it will be really useful to know all about it now.

On a sunny day, have you ever noticed how hot it can get inside a car if all the windows are closed? This is because the sun's warm rays are passing through the glass into the car, but that heat is then not being allowed to escape. The glass has trapped the heat inside and the longer you leave it without winding down the windows, the more the heat builds up. This is why you mustn't leave a dog in a car without making sure one of the windows is open, even just a little.

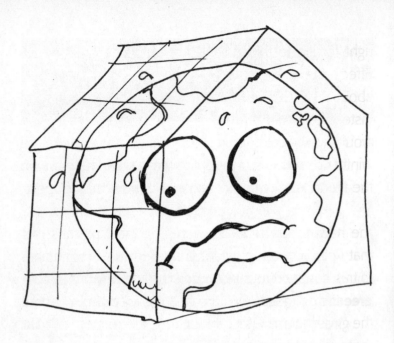

Now imagine that this is happening to the whole world. The sun's warming rays are entering the Earth's atmosphere, but instead of them all bouncing straight back out into space, a lot of this heat from the sun ends up being trapped in the atmosphere. This is called the Greenhouse Effect because the process is similar (although not exactly the same) to what happens inside a greenhouse (the glass house where gardeners keep their plants) or inside a car on a hot day.

The Greenhouse Effect is a very important natural process and is what makes the Earth such a wonderful place for plants and animals to live. It keeps the temperature just

WILL JELLYFISH RULE THE WORLD?

right for life to thrive. If there wasn't any Greenhouse Effect, the average temperature on Earth would be about 33°C COLDER than it is now. That would mean instead of hot sunny days in the middle of summer, we would have ice-cold days instead. And the middle of winter would be so cold that it would be like living on the North Pole (without the polar bears).

The reason why our atmosphere – the layer of gases that wrap around the surface of our planet – manages to trap some of the sun's warm rays is due to the various **greenhouse gases** within the atmosphere. They act like the glass that makes a car heat up on a sunny day. When the sun's rays reach our atmosphere after travelling all the way from the sun, some of them bounce straight back out into space after hitting the reflective surface

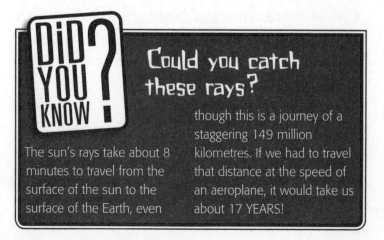

DiD YOU KNOW?

Could you catch these rays?

The sun's rays take about 8 minutes to travel from the surface of the sun to the surface of the Earth, even though this is a journey of a staggering 149 million kilometres. If we had to travel that distance at the speed of an aeroplane, it would take us about 17 YEARS!

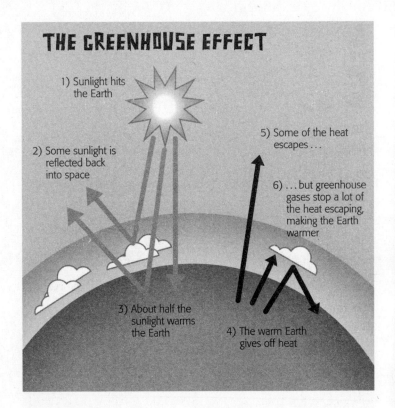

THE GREENHOUSE EFFECT

1) Sunlight hits the Earth

2) Some sunlight is reflected back into space

3) About half the sunlight warms the Earth

4) The warm Earth gives off heat

5) Some of the heat escapes ...

6) ... but greenhouse gases stop a lot of the heat escaping, making the Earth warmer

of white clouds, as well as land covered in snow and ice. However, some of the rays get absorbed by the sea, which warms the water up. The same happens on land, too.

But it's the greenhouse gases in the atmosphere that help to keep a lot of this heat within the atmosphere and stop it from escaping back out into space. It's a bit like having a blanket wrapped around the Earth – but less itchy.

The basket of greenhouse gases

The greenhouse gases make up only a tiny part of the atmosphere – about 1 per cent, the rest being made up of the gases nitrogen and oxygen – but they play a huge role in determining the temperature at the planet's surface. When scientists talk about these gases together, they call them the 'basket' of greenhouse gases.

Too many greenhouse gases and it can get too warm. Too few and it can get too chilly. There are quite a few greenhouse gases, but here are the most important . . .

WATER VAPOUR

When a kettle boils, you will see steam rising up towards the ceiling. This is water vapour. You can also see water vapour rising up above a warm bath, and if you look out of your window you will see clouds in the sky. These are made of water vapour, too.

Water vapour is water that has evaporated by being heated up, which turns it into a gas. This is how the sun can heat up the surface of large expanses of water, such as a lake or the sea, and create large clouds above. But some of these clouds – depending on how high and thick they are – can also trap the sun's heat. In fact, **water vapour** is the most significant of all the greenhouse gases and is thought to be responsible for up to 70 per cent of the Greenhouse Effect on our planet.

Without clouds we also wouldn't have any rain – and our planet would be a very, very different place. This is a good reason to love water vapour. We need greenhouse gases – just not too many!

that's water to you and me!

WILL JELLYFISH RULE THE WORLD?

CARBON DIOXIDE

Fffffffttttttttzzzzzzz. That's the sound you get when you open a bottle or can of fizzy drink. The thing that's causing that sound is all the carbon dioxide trapped inside rushing out. Fizzy drinks are made with carbonated water, which is water that has the gas carbon dioxide dissolved into it under pressure. When you breathe out, you are also exhaling carbon dioxide from your lungs.

But it isn't fizzy drinks or heavy breathing that are causing climate change. A far, far greater amount of carbon dioxide is being produced when we burn fossil fuels such as petrol or oil. In fact, whenever you burn any organic material (a substance that was once 'alive') – wood, for example – it produces carbon dioxide.

Plants turn carbon dioxide back into oxygen through their leaves – some of it gets absorbed by the sea, too – but we are now burning so much fossil fuel that there is about 40 per cent more carbon dioxide in the atmosphere today than there was before the start of the Industrial Age, which began about 200 years ago. Before it was dug up the carbon dioxide had been locked deep under the ground for millions of years.

Unlocking all this carbon dioxide so quickly is a big, big problem. Carbon dioxide helps the atmosphere absorb heat from the sun, which is why scientists are worried that too much of it is gradually increasing temperatures around the world. We have upset the natural balance of carbon dioxide entering and leaving the atmosphere. This is why we urgently need to stop burning so many fossil fuels.

METHANE

Methane is a gas that is colourless (you can't see it), odourless (you can't smell it) and flammable (it will catch fire if you light a match near it). It is created when organic matter – plants, wood, dead animals – rots or decomposes underground or underwater. Tiny bacteria produce this methane as they munch their way through this organic feast. Mmmmmm. (Methane is very useful to humans – the gas used to light a gas oven is mostly methane, but a special smell is added to it so that people can tell if there's been a leak.)

Methane only accounts for a small percentage of the volume of greenhouse gases in the atmosphere but it is very powerful – about 22 times more so than carbon dioxide – which means that it is thought to account for about 20 per cent of the Greenhouse Effect. Since the start of the Industrial Age the concentration of methane in the atmosphere has increased by about two and a half times. But it doesn't stay in the atmosphere for as

AMAZING FACTS! Operation Cow Fart

When cows munch on grass, they also swallow lots of air. This is a big problem, as this air passes through their body – including their FOUR stomachs – and is released at the other end in the form of a big fart. (Cows also burp an awful lot, too!) Scientists worry about this because cow farts and burps contain a lot of methane and this all adds to the Greenhouse Effect. This methane is produced inside the cow's tummy when all the grass it eats is being digested. In fact, cow farts could be responsible for about 5 per cent of all man-made – or should that be cow-made? – greenhouse gases! That's because there are a lot of cows: 1.5 billion cows on the planet. That's one cow for every four people.

But, in 2008, some Japanese scientists said they had an answer to the problem – a special pill that neutralizes the methane being produced inside the cow. Maybe they need to invent a fart pill for us humans, too!

PARRRP!!!

long as carbon dioxide, which can last for up to 200 years. Methane remains within the atmosphere only for about 10 years or so before turning into water vapour.

AMAZING FACTS!

The World's Biggest Fart – and why it led to humans walking the Earth

Some scientists think that if the climate gets too warm it could release millions of tonnes of methane that, at the moment, is trapped underneath the sea floor. Down there, underneath the huge weight of the water above, the methane is solid, not a gas, and is known as 'methane ice'.

Nearly 56 million years ago, the Earth experienced a period of very rapid warming – the global temperature rose 6°C in about 20,000 years. Some scientists believe this was caused by methane ice 'melting' – possibly because of a big volcanic eruption – and entering the atmosphere.

There was some good to come of this, though: it created the right conditions for some new mammals to thrive, such as the very first horses and primates (humans, monkeys, orang-utans, gorillas, chimpanzees, etc.).

WILL JELLYFISH RULE THE WORLD?

NITROUS OXIDE - NO LAUGHING MATTER

Have you ever heard of 'laughing gas'? Dentists used to use it to make patients feel happy and laugh when they were having their teeth pulled out. It stopped them from thinking about the pain. Well, the proper name for it is nitrous oxide and of all the greenhouse gases it is the fourth-largest man-made contributor to global warming. Even though there is far less of it in the atmosphere compared to other gases such as carbon dioxide, it

ASTOUNDING SCIENCE! Now, that's magic!

Some magicians perform a special trick in which they use 'invisible water' to float a small boat made out of tin foil inside a large glass jar. It looks like the boat is floating in thin air! But the secret – don't tell anyone! – is that the boat is actually 'floating' on a layer of very heavy, invisible gas called sulphur hexafluoride. But as well as being known for being used by clever magicians, it is also known as the most powerful greenhouse gas. It is a whopping 22,200 times more powerful than carbon dioxide and stays in the atmosphere for 3,200 years. Luckily, only a relatively small amount is produced each year – about 8,000 tonnes – for use by the electronics industry. But given how much impact it has, it would be better if they stopped using it and made it disappear altogether. Just like a magician!

has 296 times more impact than CO_2 and stays in the atmosphere for about 100 years.

One of the biggest man-made causes of nitrous oxide entering the atmosphere is farming. When farmers plough fields, and then spread fertilizers and muck on them to help crops grow bigger and faster, it produces nitrous oxide. It is also produced when we make nylon – a type of material used to make clothes – in factories.

OZONE

Ozone is a special type of oxygen known as an **allotrope** (it has three oxygen atoms instead of 'normal' oxygen's two – this is why it's known as O_3 instead of O_2). But whereas oxygen is essential for life – it is in the air and we need to breathe it into our lungs to live – ozone can be a dangerous form of pollution. There is a lot of ozone high up in the atmosphere – between 10km and 50km above the ground – in an area called the **ozone layer**. This is good because it protects us from some of the sun's most harmful rays that would otherwise burn our skin. But down on the ground, ozone is a problem. When sunlight hits the pollution from road traffic it creates something called 'smog' (it's that dirty-looking cloud that you can sometimes see sitting over some polluted cities on a hot day) and inside this smog is lots of ozone. This is bad for your health if you breathe it in, but it also acts as a greenhouse gas, too.

HALOCARBONS

Halocarbon describes a special group of pollutants that include some with very, very long names, such as chlorofluorocarbons (CFCs), hydrofluorocarbons (HFCs) and perfluorocarbons (PFCs). We use these gases in lots of ways including in refrigerators, aerosol spray cans and cleaning products. But they are very powerful greenhouse gases. CFCs are 10,600 times more powerful than carbon dioxide and can stay in the atmosphere for 100 years. Some halocarbons can stay in the atmosphere for **thousands** of years, so even if we stopped using them tomorrow they would remain up there for many centuries.

The good news is that in the 1980s scientists realized that halocarbons can be very damaging to the environment and managed to persuade politicians around the world that some of the worst ones should be banned. As a result, CFCs are now not used because they were found to be causing a hole in the ozone layer. People in countries close to the hole, such as New Zealand, were getting very sunburnt. The hole in the ozone layer is now slowly starting to mend itself – showing that, when we really want to, we can sort out our problems.

Greenhouse gases might make up only a relatively small part of our atmosphere but, as we will later see, it's hugely important that we monitor and keep them under control. If we don't, we risk the same fate as the flower left inside a greenhouse on a hot day. The rapid build-up of heat could lead us to wilt and even endanger our very survival.

A black and white issue: the importance of albedo

Have you ever noticed how hot dark surfaces can get in direct sunshine? Just think how hot a road surface can get on a bright summer's day. You could burn your feet if you didn't have shoes on.

The reason why this happens is due to **albedo** – a term used to describe how much an object reflects or absorbs light from the sun. In general, the whiter an object is, the more light it reflects, whereas the darker it is the more light it absorbs. Albedo is a Latin word for 'whiteness'.

Albedo plays a very important role within the atmosphere – and hence the global climate – because it helps to determine how much energy from the sun is absorbed by the atmosphere and land, and how much is reflected

AMAZING FACTS! The sliding scale of albedo

The albedo – or light reflectivity – of an object is measured on a scale between 0 and 1. '0' represents something that is completely black and reflects no light whatsoever – theoretically impossible. '1' represents something that is completely white and reflects all the light that hits it – again, theoretically impossible. Even the freshest of snow isn't completely white . . .

Surface	Albedo
Asphalt roads	0.04 – 0.12
Forests	0.05 – 0.10
Cities	0.05 – 0.20
Grass	0.05 – 0.30
Soil	0.17
Sea ice	0.30 – 0.45
Desert sand	0.40
Snow	0.60 – 0.90
Thick clouds	0.60 – 0.90
Average albedo of the Earth	**0.37**

back out into space. The ice caps, for example, reflect a huge amount of light and warmth back into space. If they disappeared, then much more of the sun's energy would be absorbed by the atmosphere, heating it up in the process. Bright white clouds, such as cumulus clouds (the big fluffy ones),

OOWW! OW! OW!

also reflect a lot of energy back out of the atmosphere. The oceans, however, have a low albedo and therefore absorb a lot of energy from the sun.

WILL JELLYFISH RULE THE WORLD?

A natural balance between all these surfaces has helped to create the temperatures we experience today, but if we significantly alter these – say, by chopping down rainforests, or causing more polar melting – then we run the very real risk of altering the planet's temperature too.

AMAZING FACTS! The biggest bang on Earth

In 1883, the largest volcanic eruption in human history occurred. A small volcanic island called Krakatoa, which lay between Java and Sumatra, two of Indonesia's biggest and most populated islands, blew up, sending 25 cubic kilometres of rock and ash into the sky above and creating the loudest noise any human has ever heard. It was even heard in Australia – 3,000km away! Two-thirds of the island was completely destroyed. So much ash entered the atmosphere that it blocked out some of the sun's rays for years afterwards. In fact, the average temperature around the world fell by about 1°C in the following year.

For a few months after the eruption, people all around the world said they saw really strange blood-red sunsets. This was due to all the ash still floating around in the atmosphere.

Where does all that carbon dioxide come from?

Of all the greenhouse gases within the atmosphere, scientists tend to pay most attention to the levels of carbon dioxide. These are rising fast and could therefore disturb the atmosphere's balance. But it's important to realize that there are many, many ways carbon dioxide enters the atmosphere, some of which are perfectly natural . . .

Respiration: When animals and micro-organisms 'breathe' they release carbon dioxide into the air. Plants neutralize this carbon dioxide by using the power of sunlight to absorb it in their leaves and turn it into oxygen, which can then be breathed in again as air. This process – when plants turn carbon dioxide into oxygen – is known as **photosynthesis**. All life depends on this crucial 'circle of life'.

Volcanoes: When a volcano erupts it releases a huge quantity of hot ash and gas, including carbon dioxide, into the atmosphere.

Forest fires: When forests catch fire in hot summers and burn, they release lots of carbon dioxide into the atmosphere. Some fires start naturally – lightning strikes, for example – but some are started by humans either by accident or on purpose.

Animal and plant waste: When a dead animal or plant decomposes (rots away), carbon dioxide is created, as well as other gases such as methane, caused by micro-organisms eating the remains.

Weathering: When rain and wind strike rocks over the course of many years, these rocks slowly start to erode. This process releases carbon dioxide that has been trapped inside the rocks for millions of years.

However, the sources of carbon dioxide that are now fast rising, and which scientists fear could radically alter our climate, are not part of the natural cycle at all. To understand why climate change has become the most important issue of our times, we have to look at the sources of carbon dioxide – and other greenhouse gases – that we ourselves are emitting at great quantities into the atmosphere. It's time to turn the spotlight on us humans and learn why we are largely responsible for the changes now occurring in our climate – many of which must stop.

3

OUR IMPACT ON THE CLIMATE

For millions of years our planet's climate has changed, sometimes dramatically, and it will continue to do so for many millions of years to come. But over the past couple of centuries, a new influence has tipped the balance and triggered a rapid and unprecedented rise in global temperatures. Over the past few decades, we've slowly started to realize that the culprit is, in fact, us – human beings! By burning huge quantities of fossil fuels to power our cars, heat our homes and make all our 'stuff', we have allowed huge amounts of greenhouse gases to enter the atmosphere.

Why the finger is pointing at us

Our intelligence is what sets us apart from the rest of the animals on this planet. (Oh, and our opposable thumbs too.) Think about it: what other animal has built skyscrapers, put representatives of their species on the moon, or developed a game in which you have to try to kick a ball into a net more times than the opposing team over the course of 90 minutes?!

But what we didn't realize was that by burning fossil fuels to give us the energy to make and use things, we were inadvertently causing a great deal of climate-altering pollution. Scientists have only started to realize in the past few decades quite how dangerous this pollution could be in terms of altering the natural balance of our atmosphere. We realize that we must now undo the problems we've created. But understanding the problems we face has been a slow process . . .

WILL JELLYFISH RULE THE WORLD?

What do a glacier and a canary have in common?

One is a massive lump of ice slowly sliding down a mountain and the other a small yellow-green bird that likes to feed on cuttlefish. How can there possibly be any connection between the two?

The reason why the two are often mentioned in the same sentence is because climatologists see the world's glaciers as the proverbial 'canaries down the mine'.

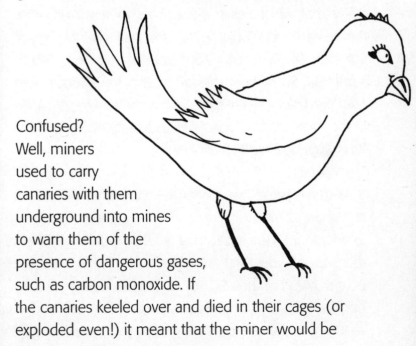

Confused?
Well, miners
used to carry
canaries with them
underground into mines
to warn them of the
presence of dangerous gases,
such as carbon monoxide. If
the canaries keeled over and died in their cages (or exploded even!) it meant that the miner would be

well advised to run for the nearest exit! So when we refer to 'canaries', it can be used as a metaphor for a warning sign.

Glaciers are one of the best visual indications anywhere in the world that our climate is rapidly changing. The fact that glaciers all around the world are melting at such a fast pace tells us that the temperatures are increasing. Glaciers have, in fact, been 'in retreat' (as climatologists like to say) since about 1850, when the Little Ice Age ended, but in the past couple of decades there appears to have been a noticeable acceleration in this retreat, which ties in with a rise in the average global temperature. Similarly, the sea ice that covers much of the Arctic Sea has been reducing in size rapidly in recent summers. So much so, in fact, that some scientists are now predicting that there could be no summer sea ice in the Arctic AT ALL within a decade – the first time this has happened for 700,000 years!

But besides these icy canaries there are other indications that show us that our climate is changing fast. Just go up to any adult – the older they are, the better – and ask them to tell you what summers and winters were like in their own childhood. They'll often talk about the long, hot summers and crisp, snowy winters they enjoyed as children: evidence enough that our seasons are changing dramatically. In the Arctic, for example, spring is now arriving about two weeks earlier than it did just a decade ago. In the UK, the first bumble-bee sightings of the year are being recorded in early January (in the 1920s late February would have been the earliest sighting), and all over Britain traditional 'spring' flowers such as daffodils are being seen as early as Christmas.

DID YOU KNOW?

Helping to track the seasons

The study of the changing seasons is called phenology. Each year, thousands of volunteers around Britain keep their own records about key tell-tale signs that the seasons are changing. These include what date the first swallows arrive, when the first blackberries appear, sightings of certain types of caterpillar and when the horse chestnut tree develops its first leaves. All this information is then collected together to create a very accurate record that is useful to scientists studying climate change. If you want to be a phenologist, then find out how by visiting **www.naturedetectives.org.uk**

One of the most noticeable aspects of our rapidly changing seasons in Britain has been the reduction in snowfall in many regions. The snowy scenes on Christmas cards now seem an unfamiliar concept to many children today who have often experienced only a light dusting of snow once or twice a winter, whereas in decades gone by January and February would usually guarantee a deep covering of snow throughout most parts of Britain, even if it was just for a few days or weeks.

Similar symptoms of shifting seasons and changing climates are being reported all over the world – longer, drier summers in the USA and Australia, or more temperate, wetter winters in Europe. Such changes have occurred countless times throughout the history of this planet, as we have seen, but what concerns scientists is that they should not be happening at such an unprecedented fast pace and that the signs are growing stronger all the time that for the very first time in history the changes are the direct result of the actions of one species – human beings!

What's causing our climate to change now?

Lots of things, is the shortest answer. Nothing ever stays still on Earth. It's a place of constant movement and change. I don't recommend that you look at a rock for a few hours and expect it to change shape. You will get more than a bit bored waiting and end up disappointed. But a human lifetime, let alone a day, is virtually insignificant

Rock

Much Later...

change

no change

compared to the overall geological timescale of this planet. If you had the time and patience to study that rock for a million years – you might want to find yourself a chair – then you would start to notice changes occurring. For a start, it would be eroded by the rain, frost and wind. It might even be covered by ice or sea.

Just because we don't notice the world around us – the trees, the coastline, the rivers – changing in form from day to day, doesn't mean that it's not doing so. The same is very much true with our climate. Our climate has changed repeatedly through the ages – and it is still doing so today. There are many things that have acted to create it – ocean currents, El Niño, altitude, the Milankovitch Cycles, etc. – but there are also things that can help it to change rapidly, too.

Perhaps the most dramatic of all the 'natural' causes of climate change are when objects, such as comets and meteors, collide with the Earth at great speed and cause a huge explosion. Even an object just a few hundred metres across in size could trigger a major change in global climatic conditions, should it hit the Earth. Luckily, this has had a habit of happening only once every 20–30 million years throughout the history of the planet. Astronomers are always on the look-out with their telescopes for any large objects coming our way, but so far they haven't spotted any. Let's keep our fingers crossed – and do let them know if you see anything.

The other cause of significant, rapid changes in global climatic conditions is volcanic eruptions. These can be dramatic events, sometimes destroying the volcano and its immediate surroundings, but they tend to affect the climate for only a few years afterwards. The last major volcanic eruption to have such an effect was Mount Pinatubo in the Philippines, which erupted in June 1991. The average global temperature fell by 0.5°C for a few months after the eruption due to the huge amount of rock and ash that it sent into the atmosphere, which partially blocked out the sun. Overall, the atmospheric effects of the eruption were felt for about three years.

Solar variations are also often linked to changes in the global climate. This is a way to describe the subtle variations in the amount of energy the Earth receives from the sun. The Earth's atmosphere normally receives 1,366 watts of energy – equivalent to 13 bright light-bulbs – per square metre. But there is currently an 11-year cycle of sunspots appearing and disappearing on the surface of the sun, the most active period for 8,000 years. Sunspots are dark patches on its surface and when they appear they can minutely dim the amount of electromagnetic radiation – light and heat – that is emitted by the sun. Even though they can reduce the energy by as little as 0.1 per cent, this reduction can

AMAZING FACTS! Solar acne

The temperature on the surface of the sun is about 5,000°C, whereas the temperature of a sunspot is 4,000°C. This 1,000°C difference is what helps to make a sunspot look darker to the eye. But don't be fooled – 4,000°C is still hot enough to melt a diamond, the hardest known natural substance.

WILL JELLYFISH RULE THE WORLD?

still alter the Earth's climate. By quite how much, no one is completely sure, although scientists think the effect over the past 400 years or so has been minimal when compared to other factors. Also, the rapid climatic changes recorded over the past couple of decades have coincided with a slight reduction in the number of sunspots appearing on the surface of the sun.

So if there haven't been any objects from outer space crashing into us, big volcanic eruptions or significant solar variations in recent times, what else could have upset the balance of our atmosphere to help cause the global climate to suddenly and rapidly warm? Look no further than a mirror. You are looking at one of the causes – **yourself**. Every one of the six billion people on this planet is affecting the climate in their own small way by living lives that are highly reliant on fossil fuels. By burning these fuels, we are releasing many millions of tonnes of carbon dioxide, and other greenhouse gases, into the atmosphere each year. But where does all this carbon dioxide come from? And what are we doing to cause it to be pumped into the atmosphere?

The dirty truth: human sources of CO_2

Transport: When we burn oil in the form of petrol, diesel and kerosene, we are releasing carbon dioxide into the atmosphere that was buried underground for millions of years. This is tipping the balance of how much carbon dioxide the atmosphere can normally contain without the Greenhouse Effect being thrown off-balance. So every time we travel by car, train, bus, ship or plane, we are causing more pollution.

Deforestation: Many rainforests around the world in countries like Brazil and Indonesia are being chopped down to use as timber, or to clear the ground for farming. The quickest and easiest way to clear the land is to use a technique called 'slash and burn', which means trees are cut down and then burned. These fires release a lot of carbon dioxide – and also stop these forests from absorbing carbon dioxide through their leaves.

Farming: We have farmed the land for thousands of years but in the past fifty years or so farmers have started to use huge quantities of fertilizers and pesticides to try to boost their harvests. It takes a lot of fossil fuels to make these products, as well as to drive the tractors that

WILL JELLYFISH RULE THE WORLD?

are used to spread them across the fields. Farmers also rear a lot of livestock nowadays for meat. Compared to using land to grow crops such as wheat and maize, rearing livestock such as cows, chickens and pigs on it is a lot more energy intensive.

Power stations and factories: There are many ways to produce the electricity that powers our lights and appliances, but by far the most popular method is still to burn fossil fuels in a large power station. Similarly, the factories that produce all the stuff we buy – clothes, DVDs, bikes, etc. – tend to be powered by electricity generated from burning fossil fuels.

The carbon cycle

The amount of carbon dioxide that naturally transfers between the atmosphere and all the world's plants and oceans is about **20 times greater** than that created by humans through burning fossil fuels and destroying rainforests.

But this naturally transferring carbon dioxide is in near-perfect balance due to the **carbon cycle**. It is the carbon dioxide being created by human activities, such as driving cars and making electricity, that is knocking the carbon cycle off-balance and increasing the amount of carbon dioxide in the atmosphere.

Photosynthesis

Dead organisms & waste products

WILL JELLYFISH RULE THE WORLD?

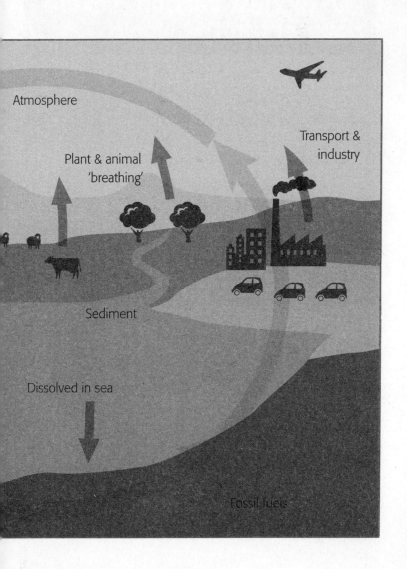

Atmosphere

Plant & animal 'breathing'

Transport & industry

Sediment

Dissolved in sea

Fossil fuels

The biggest carbon dioxide polluters in the world

Some scientists think that China might now have overtaken the United States as the biggest source of carbon dioxide pollution in the world. China, which has more people than any other country in the world – just over **1.3 BILLION** people – is developing very fast. This means that it is building lots of new factories, buildings and power stations so that its people can live the type of life enjoyed by Europeans and Americans. They also want to own cars, have bigger houses and eat new foods, particularly meat. This means China is producing more and more carbon dioxide emissions every year.

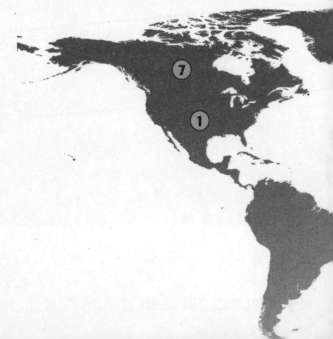

Rank	Country	National CO_2 emissions per year (tonnes)	CO_2 emissions per citizen per year (tonnes)
1	United States	1,650,020,000	20.40
2	China	1,366,654,000	3.84*
3	Russia	415,951,000	10.50
4	India	366,301,000	1.20*
5	Japan	343,117,000	9.84
6	Germany	220,596,000	9.79
7	Canada	174,401,000	20.00
8	United Kingdom	160,179,000	9.79
9	South Korea	127,007,000	9.77
10	Italy	122,726,000	7.69

* Although China and India are in the top four, look how much less pollution each person in those two countries creates, compared to people living in places such as the USA.

United States Energy Department's Carbon Dioxide Information Analysis Centre, 2004

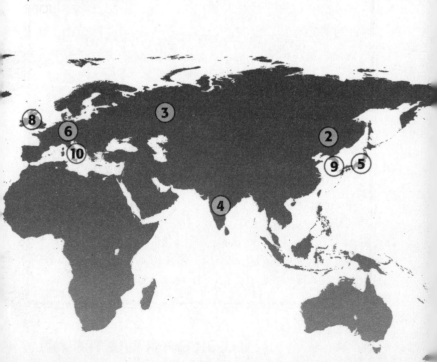

The Hockey Stick

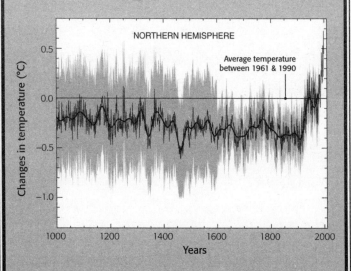

This is the famous 'Hockey Stick Graph'. It shows how much the atmosphere's average temperature has increased over the past 1,000 years in the northern hemisphere. Look how much it has risen in the past few decades compared to the steady ups and downs over the previous period. Imagine a hockey stick lying down on the ground with its 'blade' sticking up in the air – that's why scientists have given this graph its nickname. It helps us to easily see how quickly the planet is heating up compared to before the start of the Industrial Age. The fact that this 1°C rise has occurred over exactly the same period during which carbon dioxide levels have shown similar increases – due to us burning lots of fossil fuels – is a major reason why scientists believe human activity has caused much of this temperature rise.

WILL JELLYFISH RULE THE WORLD?

Two steps forward, one step back: why the Industrial Revolution solved so many problems – and created brand-new ones

It is hard to talk about climate change without talking about the Industrial Revolution. This was the moment in our history when people stopped making and growing things themselves by hand and started to get machines to help them do these jobs instead. This big change started about 300 or so years ago and it helped to create the world we know today, where we have cars, aeroplanes, factories and big cities. Before then many people grew their own food and lived in the countryside on small farms. Not many people were lucky enough to go to school and there were a lot of diseases and illnesses about.

But the Industrial Revolution meant that more people could now earn money and have more spare time to do things other than working all day long. Slowly, over the course of many years, living standards for most people started to improve and more children were able to go to school, live in cleaner, stronger houses and eat better food.

A handful of important new inventions helped to trigger the start of the Industrial Revolution. In the 1760s, a man from Lancashire called James Hargreaves invented a machine called the 'Spinning Jenny'. It made the process of making cotton thread much, much faster and, in time, it led to the building of lots of textile factories in Britain and then across the world in places such as India.

Another invention that changed people's lives was the modern iron foundry. Massive improvements were made to the iron-making process due to the introduction of coke, a special type of coal. Before this time, charcoal had been used to power furnaces used to make iron, which was much less powerful than coke because it was made from wood. The first coke-fuelled furnace

WILL JELLYFISH RULE THE WORLD?

used to make iron was built in 1709, at Coalbrookdale in Shropshire, by a man called Abraham Darby. This change meant that iron was much quicker and cheaper to make, and it quickly became the main material for building larger and stronger things such as ships, machinery and buildings. Before this time, wood had been the more usual material. Without iron we wouldn't now be able to have big things such as skyscrapers, juggernauts and really long bridges.

At about the same time as coke furnaces, the first steam engines were also being constructed. These machines used burning coal to turn water into steam, which then, using steam pressure, helped to turn big pistons inside engines. Steam engines meant that really heavy things that humans or horses couldn't push, pull or lift before could now be moved. This amazing invention led to the first tractors, the first steamboats, the first trains, the first lifts and lots of other useful things. Steam engines totally revolutionized the world and made humans realize that they could use fossil fuels, such as coal and oil, as a useful form of energy that saved them having to do these big, difficult jobs themselves.

But even though these inventions helped to change the world, they also introduced a new problem – one that it took us many years to realize even existed. Because we were now burning lots more fossil fuels, we were producing lots more pollution. Some people realized this was a problem straight away because it meant that most big cities had horrible, dirty skies and all the buildings became covered in soot and dirt. It also got into people's lungs and made them very ill.

However, it has only been in the past 40 years or so that scientists have realized that all this pollution – particularly the carbon dioxide – entering the atmosphere is also changing the climate, too.

Fossil fuels – the burning issue of our age

Many millions of years ago, a long time before humans existed on Earth, there were animals and plants living on this planet just like there are today. But it was a very strange-looking place. On the land, there were big swamps filled with large trees and ferns. The seas were awash with a green slime called algae.

But all these living things shared one thing in common: in the end, they all died. And it's what became of them after they died that's so important to the story of fossil fuels. This time in the Earth's history was called the **Carboniferous Period** and scientists say it can be dated to about 360 to 286 million years ago.

Over the course of millions of years, the remains of all these dead animals and plants built up either at the bottom of the sea, or under the ground. For example, some animals and plants died and quickly got covered in mud. In these airless conditions – and under the extreme pressure and heat that occur under the sea-bed or ground – these remains slowly started to turn into fossil fuels, such as coal, oil or gas.

Millions of years later some of these fuels then started to rise towards the surface again. This is because the Earth's 'crust' – the 10–30-km-thick 'hard' surface of the Earth's outer shell – bends, twists and distorts over long periods of time, causing oil and gas to 'float' towards the surface because they are lighter than the rocks around them. Coal was forced towards the surface as the rocks around it rubbed and knocked against it.

About 5,000 years ago, humans started to notice that fossil fuels could be found under the ground. But it wasn't until the start of the Industrial Revolution that we began to realize that these fuels could be incredibly useful to us. And coal was the first fossil fuel that we started to burn in vast quantities . . .

COAL

The first deposits of coal were found in China about 10,000 years ago. At the time, people thought it was a magical stone that could burn. (They were basically right.)

Coal is a black/brown-coloured rock and is found in many places around the world, including Russia, the USA, China, Australia and India, where it has to be dug out of the ground, usually by miners.

WILL JELLYFISH RULE THE WORLD?

Many homes in Britain used to burn coal in their fireplaces to keep warm in the winter. But in the 1950s all the smoke from these coal fires was starting to cause dense fogs during winter in some of the larger cities such as London. People used to call these fogs 'pea-soupers' because they were as thick as pea soup! Sometimes you could hardly see your hand in front of you. A law was introduced called the Clean Air Act, which banned people from burning coal in some areas.

However, coal is still used today in huge quantities to make electricity at power stations. The largest coal-fired power station in Europe is called **Drax** and is located in Yorkshire. It produces 7 per cent of all the electricity used in Britain and it is the single biggest source of carbon dioxide in the country.

Scientists think there is enough coal still in the ground to last another few hundred years. But this could be a big problem: coal is the most polluting of all the fossil fuels. Many countries are trying to cut back on their use of coal because it is so polluting. But others, most notably China and India, are using ever larger amounts of coal each year to make their electricity.

OIL

Oil is what makes the world go around. Well, the human world at least. It is hard to imagine what life would be like without oil as it has completely transformed the human experience on this planet. Oil allows us to drive in cars, fly in aeroplanes and much, much more besides. The easiest way to understand why it has been so useful to humans is to think of it as a liquid that is both transportable and contains a relatively huge amount of energy. Imagine driving a car that ran on coal. You would have to shovel all the coal into the car and then try to light it. Equally, try to imagine driving a car that ran on wood. Oil, by comparison, allows us to travel much longer distances at far greater speeds than any of our ancestors.

But oil must first be processed into petrol, diesel or kerosene before it is of any use to us. The black sticky stuff they dig out of the ground is called **crude oil** and is a long way from the liquid available at the petrol station. The process to **refine** crude oil into useful fuels, such as petrol, wasn't invented until the 1850s.

Until that point – and for quite a long period afterwards – coal was by far the more popular fossil fuel. But once people knew how to make petrol, commercial oil wells were soon to follow, with the first being built in Romania in 1857. Oil finally overtook coal as the world's most important fossil fuel in the 1950s and its use has continued to grow ever since.

There are three main fuels derived from crude oil. All of them are produced by a process called **distillation**, which is a method of separating mixtures by heating them in a special tank . . .

AMAZING FACTS!

Oil strike at Hit

The very first discovery of oil was made 5,000 years ago. It was discovered seeping from the ground at a place called Tuttul, which today is called 'Hit' and is found in modern-day Iraq.

The Egyptians used to use crude oil – oil that hasn't yet been **refined** into, say, petrol – as a medicine to heal wounds. Native Americans used to use crude oil to treat frost-bite. And until recently, many people used to wash with a soap made from coal tar. If you look hard enough, you can still find it in some shops today.

WILL JELLYFISH RULE THE WORLD?

Petrol/gasoline: About 70 per cent of the world's petrol is used to power vehicles; the rest is used to make plastics and as a heating fuel. Every day, about one trillion litres of petrol are consumed around the world – 44 per cent of which is used up by Americans.

Diesel: Used in diesel engines, which historically have been used to power larger vehicles such as trucks and trains. However, lots of cars are now powered by diesel too.

Kerosene: Used to produce the fuel used in aeroplanes, as well as for heating homes in rural areas that are too remote to connect to mains supplies.

WORLD'S TOP OIL PRODUCERS, 2006

(thousand barrels per day)

Rank	Country	Production
1	Saudi Arabia	10,665
2	Russia	9,677
3	United States	8,330
4	Iran	4,148
5	China	3,845
6	Mexico	3,707
7	Canada	3,288
8	United Arab Emirates	2,945
9	Venezuela	2,803
10	Norway	2,786
11	Kuwait	2,675
12	Nigeria	2,443
13	Brazil	2,167
14	Algeria	2,122
15	Iraq	2,008

WORLD'S TOP OIL CONSUMERS, 2006

Rank	Country	Consumption
1	United States	20,687
2	China	7,201
3	Japan	5,159
4	Russia	2,811
5	Germany	2,665
6	India	2,572
7	Canada	2,264
8	Brazil	2,217
9	South Korea	2,174
10	Saudi Arabia	2,139
11	Mexico	1,997
12	France	1,961
13	United Kingdom	1,825
14	Italy	1,732
15	Iran	1,679

US Energy Information Administration

WILL JELLYFISH RULE THE WORLD?

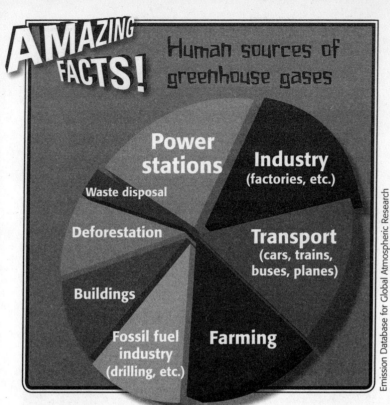

AMAZING FACTS!

Human sources of greenhouse gases

- Power stations
- Industry (factories, etc.)
- Waste disposal
- Deforestation
- Transport (cars, trains, buses, planes)
- Buildings
- Fossil fuel industry (drilling, etc.)
- Farming

Emission Database for Global Atmospheric Research

NATURAL GAS

Natural gas is a type of fossil fuel that is extracted, like coal and oil, from underground deposits. It is usually found very close to crude oil and before it had a practical use it used to be burned off in a process known as **flaring**, which is now widely banned because it is so wasteful and polluting. However, today natural gas is a very popular fuel and is used for domestic heating and cooking, as well as for powering turbines at power stations that produce electricity. Natural gas mainly consists of methane, but sometimes contains other flammable gases such as propane.

In the 1970s, Britain began to exploit newly found natural gas reserves in the North Sea, but these reserves are now running out and Britain (along with many other countries) is having to use huge ships to transport liquefied natural gas from places such as Kuwait in the Middle East, which is home to the world's largest gas field. Gas is also being imported from Russia by long pipelines stretching all the way across Europe.

How do climatologists know for sure humans are causing climate change?

They don't know for sure. Very few things in science can be proved with 100 per cent certainty. But the evidence is now overwhelming and it appears to be growing more compelling all the time. In fact, in 2007 a very large group of climatologists from around the world, called the **Intergovernmental Panel on Climate Change** (thankfully shortened to IPCC!), said it was 'very likely' that man-made greenhouse-gas emissions were causing the climate to warm. Just four years earlier the same group said that it was 'likely'. There remains

WILL JELLYFISH RULE THE WORLD?

Department for Business, Enterprise and Regulatory Reform.
Digest of United Kingdom Energy Statistics 2008

AMAZING FACTS! One million to one

The amount of fossil fuels that we now burn in just one year around the world is equal to the build-up of material from the dead animals and vegetation over a one-million-year period during the Carboniferous Era. In other words, we are now releasing into the atmosphere **each year** a volume of carbon dioxide that took **a million years** to accumulate.

Put like that, it's no wonder we are jolting the natural balance of the Earth's atmosphere.

In 2007, Britain's total energy consumed was the equivalent of 164.6 million tonnes of oil. This is how we used up all that fuel . . .

Services (farming etc.)

Industry (factories etc.)

Transport (cars, trains, buses, planes)

Domestic (heating and cooking)

a tiny minority of so-called 'sceptics' who doubt the role of humans, but the huge and ever-growing majority of scientists who have studied climate change say that we are to blame. Turn to page 212 to find out more about climatologists in the past.

Climatologists at work

IS THAT YOU?

NO, I THINK
IT'S A FOSSIL ...

TREE RINGS

If you chop down a tree and count the rings on the trunk it is possible to accurately discover the age of the tree. Some trees, such as the giant sequoias in California, have been found to be more than 3,000 years old! **Dendroclimatology**, which is the name scientists give to the study of tree rings – they love long names, don't they? – also allows them to see what the climate was like during specific times during the tree's life. This is called 'wiggle-matching'. If they see similar 'wiggles' in the rings in different trees they can try to work out if, say, the climate at that time was dry, cold or wet.

SEDIMENTARY ROCKS

To look back at what the climate was like many millions of years ago, scientists have to rely on studying rocks. Sedimentary rocks are formed over millions of years when many layers of material are slowly deposited over an area – materials such as grit and stones washing down a river, seashells building up at the bottom of an ocean, or large areas of mud drying up. A thick 'sandwich' of layers gives clues about the various types of climate during the creation of the rocks. Some layers will contain fossils of plants and animals that provide important clues to both the age of the layer and the climatic conditions.

hellooo! I've waited years for a bit of ~~dinner~~ company

ICE CORES

By drilling kilometres down to reach ice that was formed many thousands of years ago, scientists can examine the ice to discover what the atmosphere was like back then. Ice cores have helped scientists build up a very accurate picture of what the climate has been like up to 800,000 years ago.

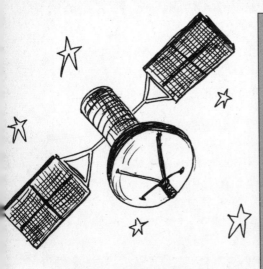

SATELLITES

There are hundreds of satellites orbiting in space around the Earth. Some allow us to communicate with each other via mobile phones and the Internet. Others take photographs of the surface of the Earth and allow scientists to record changes such as growing deserts or shrinking ice caps.

COMPUTER MODELS

Computers are excellent at working out very complicated calculations that would be impossible for humans to complete – or without spending the rest of their lives doing so, at least. Climatologists use computers to create simulations of how the climate might 'behave' across long periods of time. They can then change certain 'ingredients' such as, say, carbon dioxide levels in the atmosphere, or sea temperatures, to see how they might affect the climate. By getting the computer to repeat this process thousands of times, scientists can work out an average to see the most likely climate patterns over the coming decades.

WILL JELLYFISH RULE THE WORLD?

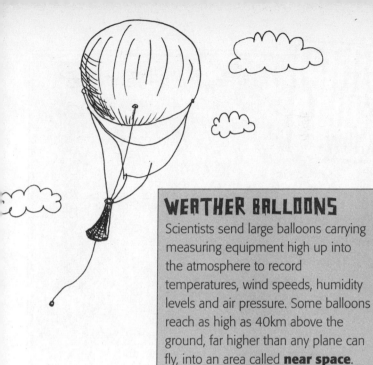

WEATHER BALLOONS

Scientists send large balloons carrying measuring equipment high up into the atmosphere to record temperatures, wind speeds, humidity levels and air pressure. Some balloons reach as high as 40km above the ground, far higher than any plane can fly, into an area called **near space**.

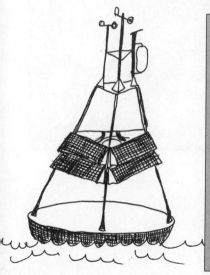

SEA BUOYS

To study the temperature of the sea and to measure ocean currents, hundreds of buoys are positioned in the world's oceans and seas. Some of them are anchored to the sea-bed, whereas others are allowed to drift in the ocean currents. They are very important for predicting and monitoring weather events such as El Niño.

How many climatologists does it take to change a light-bulb?

No, this isn't a joke. Pity really. The answer is that it has taken the combined efforts of around 3,000 climatologists since 1988 to convince the world that it needs to change its light-bulbs – and a whole lot more besides – to help save energy and thereby reduce greenhouse-gas emissions. This group of climatologists (the IPCC) is made up of scientists from all over the world. Every few years they meet up to discuss the latest research into climate change and write an assessment report, which is then given to politicians around the world so they can decide what to do. The IPCC doesn't actually conduct any research itself – it just acts like a giant panel of expert judges flicking through all the research from around the world and then painting a big picture of how the world should expect the climate to change – and what it should do to prevent further changes, or to prepare for coming changes. One of the most important recommendations made by the IPCC is to reduce the amount of energy we all use – and that includes all of us changing to low-energy light-bulbs!

So, we got there in the end. After decades of relying on fossil fuels to improve our lives in a wide variety of ways – cars, planes, heavy industry, etc. – without giving much thought to whether there were any negative consequences, we've now finally realized that it has caused some significant problems. Scientists have worked hard to prove to us that by pumping extra greenhouse gases into the atmosphere we risk disrupting the natural balance and changing our climate. We now have to decide whether to take their advice and rapidly reduce this pollution – or ignore them and face the consequences.

4

THE EFFECTS OF CLIMATE CHANGE

Now that the scientists have done the hard work and discovered that we are causing the climate to warm, we face a choice: either we ignore what they are saying and carry on polluting, or we try to reduce our pollution, as well as start adapting our lives to suit a new, warmer climate. If we choose the first option, we will have to learn to live with the many problems caused by climate change – not just for our lives, but for all the other life-forms that share this planet with us. Can we really afford to be so complacent?

Do I really need to worry about climate change?

Well, yes – you really do. At first glance, a small rise in temperatures around the world seems like nothing to worry about. This difference would be barely noticeable to most people if you asked them to describe whether, say, 25°C feels different from 24°C, particularly if they're sitting on a beach licking their ice creams. They would just say that it's hot – and very pleased they'd be too!

But even just a single degree rise in the average global temperature is likely to lead to some major changes on Earth that will affect not just humans, but the vast majority of life on this planet. And if the rise in temperature is even greater than is currently being forecast – scientists seem to think that a 2°C rise, at least, is very likely throughout this century if we continue to emit as much of the greenhouse gases as we do today – then we are into the world of extremes. Extreme storms, extreme heatwaves, extreme sea-level rises, extreme droughts, extreme flooding, extreme ice-cap melting. And nobody wants this to happen.

AMAZING FACTS!

Spot the difference: the incredible shrinking glaciers

Look at these two photographs of the Upsala Glacier in Argentina taken from exactly the same position. The one on the top was taken in 1928 and the one on the bottom was taken in 2004. It took just 76 years for the huge volume of ice you can see contained within the glacier to melt away – and it is still retreating today at a rate of 200 metres every year. Some scientists are predicting that due to climate change, some of the world's glaciers will have completely melted within a decade. This will be both a huge shame – they are one of nature's most wonderful sights – and a huge problem. Many people around the world rely on meltwater from glaciers for their drinking water, as these glaciers feed water to some of the world's most important rivers, such as the Ganges in India.

Why are trees getting drunk?

'Drunk trees' are already a problem in forests within the Arctic Circle. In places such as Alaska and Siberia you can experience the very strange sight of trees leaning over at funny angles. Scientists have given them the nickname of 'drunk trees' because together they look like they've all been getting a bit tipsy. But it's not because they've been drinking too much beer, that's for sure.

WILL JELLYFISH RULE THE WORLD?

Instead, there is a serious reason: these trees are an early warning sign that the polar regions on Earth are warming. Normally, these trees are anchored to the ground by their roots, set hard in the permafrost. **Permafrost** is only found in very cold places and refers to ground that is **perma**nently frozen all year round. But rising temperatures have started melting the permafrost in some areas and, as a result, trees have started to lose their support. In some places, the bodies of woolly mammoths have even started to emerge in the mushy mud after spending thousands of years frozen under the ground. People in Siberia have even been known to feed this ancient, stinking meat to their dogs!

How hot is a heatwave?

A hot day to you and me is probably just a mild day for someone living in, say, Libya or Arizona, where it can be like living inside an oven. So what is a heatwave? Officially, it's a period of hot weather in which the average maximum temperature for a region is reached on five consecutive days. If that sounds a little confusing, then some countries make it much simpler to understand by saying that a heatwave is when temperatures reach 25°C on five or more days in a row. Climatologists predict that there will be an increasing number of heatwaves over the coming decades as temperatures rise – some say the chance of a heatwave occurring has already doubled since humans began emitting greenhouse gases. Heatwaves can also happen at the same time as long droughts, causing extra problems.

Will climate change cause more hurricanes?

Not necessarily, but climatologists do expect the intensity and strength of hurricanes to increase over the coming decades. This is because hurricanes are caused by a build-up of heat and moisture within the atmosphere over the tropical regions of the planet; hence their other name – **tropical cyclones**. As temperatures rise due

AMAZING FACTS! The Great Heatwave of 2003

During 4–13 August 2003, Europe experienced one of the most extreme heatwaves since records began. In France, which was the most affected country, temperatures passed 40°C on most days in some regions, which directly led to the deaths of an estimated 15,000 people. In the UK, about 2,500 deaths were believed to have resulted from the extreme heat. Faversham in Kent saw the hottest temperature ever recorded in the UK when it reached 38.5°C on 10 August. The scorching temperatures also led to many crop failures across the Continent as plants wilted in the heat. The 2003 heatwave led many people in Europe to start talking about climate change – and fear its consequences.

What have Carol, Bob and Anita all got in common?

Don't ever be tricked by the friendly, familiar names given to hurricanes that form over the Atlantic. The US National Hurricane Center in Florida has had a tradition since the 1950s of naming every hurricane that occurs each season in an alphabetical sequence. Until 1978 it only gave them female names, but since then it has alternated between female and male names. There are six lists of names that are used in rotation. Therefore, the 2009 list will be used again in 2015. If a hurricane is particularly damaging, though, the name is 'retired' and never used again. These are some of the retired names: Andrew, Katrina, Fifi, Allison, Carol, Bob, Lili, Hazel, David, Anita, Hugo and Rita.

And here's the list of names for the 2010 hurricane season: Ana, Bill, Claudette, Danny, Erika, Fred, Grace, Henri, Ida, Joaquin, Kate, Larry, Mindy, Nicholas, Odette, Peter, Rose, Sam, Teresa, Victor, Wanda.

to global warming, the energy contained within the cyclonic weather systems that cause hurricanes to form will increase. Therefore, we are likely to witness more Category 5 hurricanes, which are the strongest and most destructive of all the weather systems the planet can throw at us. Winds reach 250km an hour and the average sea level rises more than five metres, causing both destruction due to the high winds and flooding due to the surging seas.

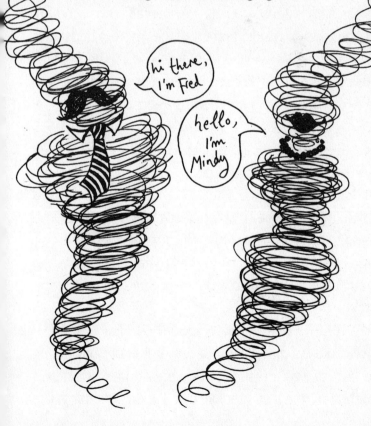

Will climate change mean we get even more rain?

It's easy to assume that climate change only means hotter, drier weather for all. But this would be wrong. Some regions of the planet will actually experience increased rainfall as global temperatures rise. In fact, the UK is predicted to be one of these areas, with increasingly intense bursts of rainfall over coming decades. As a result, there will be more floods and storm surges (when coastal waters rise during a storm, causing flooding). The overall prediction for the UK is to have warmer winters and hotter, wetter summers.

The other major impact of climate change will be sea-level rises. As the polar ice caps melt, any meltwater that was previously ice sitting on the land (as opposed to floating in the sea) will increase the overall volume of water in the oceans. This will cause sea levels to rise across the planet. Just try to think what happens when you put too much ice in a drink – it spills over the top.

There is still a lot of debate about how dramatic these rises could be, but it's worth remembering that during the last ice age the sea levels were about 130 metres lower than they are today! Don't worry, nothing like this is going to occur during our lifetime, but scientists do predict that sea levels could rise by 18–59cm over the coming century. It might not sound like a lot but it would be enough to greatly increase the risk of flooding in some of the world's most populated cities, such as London, New York and Mumbai. In fact, 13 of the world's 15 largest cities are located on coastlines.

AMAZING FACTS!

Rising tide

Tuvalu is the fourth-smallest country in the world. It is a small group of tropical islands located in the Pacific Ocean nearly 3,000km north-east of Australia. The people who live on these islands are sometimes referred to as the first victims of climate change. This is because the highest point in Tuvalu stands just five metres above sea level and any rise in sea level will threaten its people. In fact, the islanders have already made plans to evacuate to New Zealand or Fiji once the sea begins to wash over the islands, as already happens during storms and very high tides.

Will jellyfish rule the world?

Well, in terms of a straight head count against humans, they already do. There are about six and a half billion of us on this planet, whereas a **fluther** of jellyfish (or some people call a group of jellyfish a **smack**), measuring just 26 square kilometres to a depth of 11 metres, that wiped out a Northern Ireland salmon farm in 2007 was said by marine scientists to have contained **billions** of mauve stinger jellyfish.

Worse, this menacing mass of scyphozoans (the fancy name for the jellyfish family) looks set to swell further: 2008 was the eighth summer in a row that the Mediterranean coastline had been plagued by them. Traditionally, jellyfish plagues have only been a concern once every decade or so.

They are also not the only species likely to thrive as our climate changes. Coccolithophores are said to be booming as carbon dioxide levels increase and ocean temperatures rise. These single-celled algae and phytoplankton (microscopic plants) sit at the bottom of the marine food chain and have, as a result, helped other species to multiply. An expedition of marine ecologists to Antarctica in 2007 reported that higher-than-average concentrations of phytoplankton and krill (tiny shrimp-like animals) had encouraged more shrimp and fish, which, in turn, had encouraged minke whales and seabirds.

Back on shore, rats, slugs and snails, foxes, mosquitoes, wasps, cockroaches, rabbits and pigeons are already enjoying our warming climate. Shrewsbury and Atcham Borough Council in England said in 2007 that complaints about rats had doubled in just 12 months and its chief rat-catcher said climate change was partly to blame.

Here's some good news, though: nature-spotters have been reporting a rise in sightings of rare 'foreign' species such as the long-tailed blue butterfly and Cetti's warbler in the UK. Alas, neither feed on jellyfish.

Should we worry about 'frog fungus'?

In a word, yes. This isn't the name of a fancy new type of mushroom to be found in the supermarkets to liven up a stir-fry. Rather, it's a grave problem that's threatening the very survival of many frog species around the world. This powerful fungus leaves its victims so weak they become completely vulnerable to predators. Scientists are partly blaming climate change for its arrival because the fungus seems to thrive in warmer temperatures.

WILL JELLYFISH RULE THE WORLD?

Chytrid fungi have been infecting amphibians, such as frogs and toads, and causing an often fatal disease called chytridiomycosis, for the past couple of decades. This disease is spreading at a very fast pace through frog colonies around the world – covering up to 100km a year – most noticeably in Central America, where some frog species are already believed to have become extinct. There is no known cure, and once it infects a habitat 50 per cent of amphibian species and 80 per cent of individual animals will die within a year.

Amphibians are now one of the most threatened types of animal anywhere in the world, as they are particularly vulnerable to subtle changes in their natural habitats. Biologists now believe that half of the 6,000 or so known amphibian species are threatened with extinction. In fact, 165 species are thought to have already become extinct, with 35 **known** to be extinct. Perhaps the best known of the now-extinct amphibian species is the Monteverde Golden Toad that once lived in the rainforests of Costa Rica. It has not been seen since 1989 and is thought by scientists to be one of the first animal extinctions that can be blamed on global warming. The region's famous harlequin frogs have also suffered hugely over the past couple of decades, with up to two-thirds of the 110 species having vanished.

What would Darwin say? There are always winners and losers in nature, aren't there?

It's certainly right that species have come and gone over the millennia. For example, at one time the dinosaurs ruled the world, but then they suddenly disappeared and were replaced by other dominant species. In many ways, humans are the new dinosaurs in that we are now the dominant species. This is **Darwinism** in action.

Charles Darwin was a British scientist who lived during the 19th century. Darwin became famous around the world during his lifetime for coming up with the idea that the wide variety of life on Earth had evolved over many millions of years from a small group of common ancestors via a process he called **natural selection**. Today, we would call this theory **survival of the fittest**, whereby the 'failures' in any species soon die out and only the most successful of each species learn to adapt and, therefore, thrive. Over time, this leads to both new species and extinctions. Brutal and cruel, perhaps, but that's how Darwin saw life. Even though all the scientific evidence now supports Darwin's **theory of evolution**, some people still believe that God created all life on Earth – meaning that Darwin remains a controversial figure almost 130 years after his death. Just try to imagine what it must have been like when he first proposed the idea that humans and apes shared a common ancestor. Unsurprisingly, he was mocked for his revolutionary ideas.

But what would Darwin make of today's climate change? Isn't it yet another challenge for the world's species to face up to? There will be losers and there will be winners, for sure, but isn't that just the way it's always been throughout the history of life on this planet? The difference now, of course, is that it is the actions of just one species – us humans – that are threatening the survival of so many others. We are acting like bullies. Is that really a fair way to behave?

As we've seen with jellyfish, rats and mosquitoes, climate change is likely to be a blessing for some species. Warmer temperatures will offer new opportunities for these species to thrive. But climate change will alter the conditions found in most habitats around the world and, for the more vulnerable species that are less able to adapt, this could spell the end of their time on Earth.

Polar bears are often mentioned as being among the animals most vulnerable to climate change. The ice floes that surround the North Pole, their habitat, are melting fast, and once they have gone this appealing animal will have no ability to hunt for its favourite food – baby seals. It needs the ice to be able to launch surprise attacks on seals. Without the ice, it wouldn't stand a chance of catching a seal in the open water. It is highly unlikely that polar bears would adapt their diet quickly enough to survive and perhaps within a generation they would be extinct.

Ultimately, it will be the animals that are best able to adapt to their changing habitats that stand the best chance of riding out the impacts of climate change. Or it will be the animals, such as birds and fish, which are able to move away and head towards new locations that mirror the conditions found in their old habitats. This is already happening. Fish that were once found off Cornwall in southern England have now been spotted near the Shetland Islands in northern Scotland. Likewise, the mountain gamebirds called ptarmigans that were once found in the Scottish Highlands are now migrating further north to Norway.

WILL JELLYFISH RULE THE WORLD?

But some bird
species are
not moving
quickly
enough, it
seems. In
France, bird
populations moved
northwards by 91km
between 1989 and 2006
as their habitats were
altered by climate change.
But scientists say that if
they wanted to seek exactly the
same kind of habitats they once enjoyed they should
have flown 273km northwards. This shows that, over
time, some highly mobile species such as birds and
fish might still suffer from climate change because they
don't – or can't – move quickly enough.

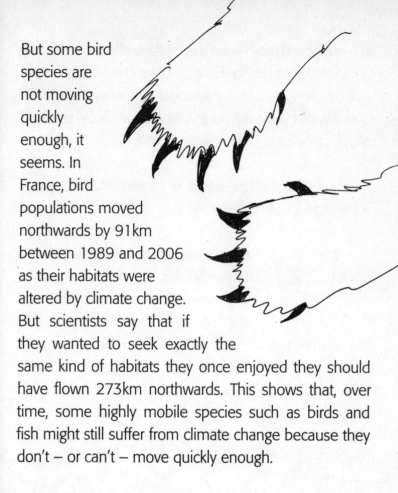

And there are other problems, too. The rapidly changing
seasons mean that some birds are suffering from
shortage of their usual food sources. For example,
the chaffinch is now laying its eggs a week earlier on
average than it did in the 1960s. But once the young
hatch, the parents are struggling to find them food
such as caterpillars because they haven't yet emerged

themselves. Sea-birds such as puffins are also struggling because they can't find their usual food source, the sand eel, which is itself being affected by the warming seas. This shows how a single jolt anywhere along the food chain can affect all the species higher up.

Here's just a small selection of species that are highly vulnerable to climate change . . .

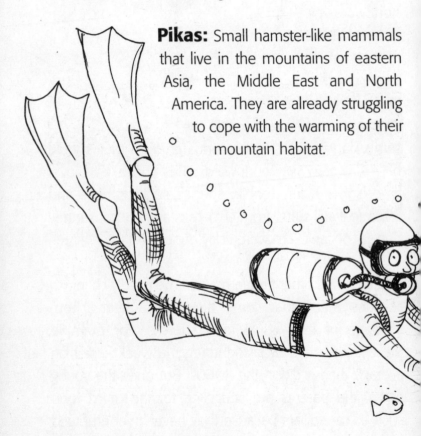

Pikas: Small hamster-like mammals that live in the mountains of eastern Asia, the Middle East and North America. They are already struggling to cope with the warming of their mountain habitat.

WILL JELLYFISH RULE THE WORLD?

Sea turtles: Sea-level rises will threaten their traditional nesting beaches.

North Atlantic right whales: Warming seas will threaten their food source.

Penguins: As the Antarctic region warms, so the usual nesting and feeding sites of penguins will be affected. Over the past 50 years, the population of emperor penguins has declined by 50 per cent, and scientists think this is down to warming temperatures.

Why we need lawnmowers under the sea

Perhaps a little clarification is required?! The Lawnmower **fish** has an important role to play cleaning green slime and seaweed from coral reefs, which are home to more than 25 per cent of all marine life. If they didn't do 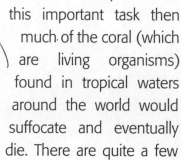 this important task then much of the coral (which are living organisms) found in tropical waters around the world would suffocate and eventually die. There are quite a few reef fish that act as 'lawnmowers' by eating algae and seaweed, but perhaps the best known is the parrotfish. It uses its jagged jaws to scrape away plant life from the coral surface.

The world's coral reefs are highly vulnerable to climate change. Warming waters and sea-level rises both threaten their survival. Some of the increasing carbon dioxide in the atmosphere is also being absorbed by the world's oceans which, in turn, is increasing the acidity of the water, further damaging the reefs. A phenomenon known as **bleaching** is already impacting many reefs around the world. This means that the coral reef is dying and in the process turning a light, lifeless colour. As the waters warm, so the coral also becomes more prone to algae building up on its surface. This is where the lawnmower fish come in. By cleaning the reefs, they help to provide some extra protection from climate change.

WILL JELLYFISH RULE THE WORLD?

Is the season over for the bluebells?

Well, it's not looking good. Bluebells are one of Britain's most famous and best-loved native flowers. We are lucky to have these beautiful flowers – Britain is home to as many as half the world's bluebells. But the early arrival of spring, brought about by climate change, is threatening the long-term survival of these flowers. They use the cold winter weather to grab an advantage over other plants that also inhabit woodland floors by flowering first. But early springs mean that other species such as cow parsley will be able to get a foothold too and possibly bully the bluebells out altogether.

In many ways, bluebells represent the problems now facing many plant species. Unlike some animals, plants can't get up and move to a new habitat should climate change make their life intolerable. Their seeds can be transported by the wind or by animals (via their droppings), but plants obviously have no control over this and tend to find it harder to adapt as quickly as some animals.

Climate change now threatens many of Britain's native plant species, not just the bluebells. And as with animals, there will be losers and winners in the plant world. In Britain, botanists have noticed that some plant species such as the lesser butterfly orchid, goldenrod and mountain pansy are already suffering. However, plants such as the bee orchid, Hart's tongue fern and prickly lettuce are actually benefiting from the warmer temperatures. A very modest increase in temperatures would probably benefit most plants in Britain, but if temperatures got too high then many would suffer. This is already happening in warmer areas of the world where the extra heat is tipping the balance. In California, botanists fear that two-thirds of the native plants will have an 80 per cent smaller area in which to live by the end of the century. And because most animals rely on plant life for their own existence this will have a knock-on effect for many animal species, too.

But perhaps the greatest threat is to the species that live for the longest amount of time – namely, trees. Trees can live for hundreds of years, sometimes longer, and young trees can take a long time to establish themselves. There is now a risk that the climate will change too rapidly for many tree species to adapt in time to the new conditions. Heatwaves and drought are a particular threat. Some people are thinking ahead, though: olive trees and vineyards are already being planted in Britain in anticipation of a warmer climate.

WILL JELLYFISH RULE THE WORLD?

Surely climate change can't be such a big problem for us humans?

Don't be so sure! It's sometimes tempting to think that humans are clever enough to solve any problem put in front of us. After all, we have a strong track record in doing just that. We've put men on the moon. We've climbed the highest mountains. We can fly to the other side of the planet in under a day. We have defeated some of the most deadly diseases. So why should we worry about climate change? Because climate change presents us with our very biggest challenge yet, as it will affect so many aspects of our lives. We have no way of protecting ourselves completely from its impact by just 'pulling up the drawbridge' and kidding ourselves that it doesn't affect us. It most certainly will – all of us.

There are two main problems associated with climate change – too much heat, and too much water. Either can be deadly but combined they will make our lives very uncomfortable and difficult, and in some situations even pose a threat to life.

FOOD

Until the day comes along when we invent special food pills – anyone for a fish and chips pill? – we will be reliant on **growing** all our food. We have had thousands of years of practice at honing these skills, and today we rely on a very complex system of food production. We now grow food all over the world and ship it great distances before it reaches our plate. Look down at the next meal you eat and guess how each ingredient has been made and where it has come from.

Today we eat tomatoes from Spain, beef from Argentina, chicken from Thailand, rice from India and apples from New Zealand. While we might still eat, say, potatoes and peas from Britain, we are increasingly reliant on food from abroad. But what happens when climate change begins to affect these foreign crops through drought, flooding and storms? What happens when pests such as locusts and white fly begin to thrive in the heat? What will happen when livestock starts to die in the heat or drown in the floods? It will impact us, of course. Food will become more expensive as crops begin to fail around the world – in fact, this is already starting to happen.

Rising food prices and failing crops will have a far bigger impact on the poorer regions of the world, such as Africa, however. Here, climate change really is a life or death

WILL JELLYFISH RULE THE WORLD?

issue. Just one failed harvest can lead to widespread famine and starvation, as has happened on so many occasions in the past.

WATER

All life on Earth relies on water to survive – and we are no different. Climate change will be a particular threat to fresh-water supplies – already at risk in many drier

AMAZING FACTS! Some clouds really do have a silver lining

In 2006, droughts across China were so severe that the government ordered special rockets to be fired into the air to make rain clouds form overhead. Using a powder called silver iodide to trigger rain has been common in some countries since the 1950s but the Chinese are the world leaders at 'rainmaking', largely because the effects of climate change, particularly frequent droughts, are already hurting China's huge population. But some environmentalists worry about the use of silver iodide because it can cause pollution when it gets washed into rivers and lakes.

regions of the world from over-use by farmers and other users, such as golf courses. A lack of fresh water will force people either to move away, or to use lots of energy and money to **desalinate** (take the salt out of) sea water. Climatologists are predicting that some areas on the planet will be virtually uninhabitable to humans in coming decades because they will become just too hot and dry. In fact, there have been predictions that a billion people – almost one in seven people on Earth today – could be forced to move home over the next 50 years in order to escape the effects of climate change. The search for adequate supplies of fresh water will be one of the greatest reasons to migrate.

FLOODING

The historic city of New Orleans in the USA was devastated by Hurricane Katrina in the summer of 2005. Thousands of people were killed when huge areas of the city were destroyed by flooding as the levees (giant walls) that were used to hold back the sea burst. The disaster was like looking at a crystal ball of the impact flooding could have around the world as storms intensify and sea levels rise due to climate change over the coming decades.

There will be very little that we can do about rising sea levels and increasing storm surges other than to move to higher ground, or to build expensive barriers. But how long will they protect us? The Thames Barrier was built in London to help protect the capital city from flooding, but many now wonder how much longer it will last before a new, bigger barrier is required. If sea levels continue to rise as predicted, then the barrier might need to be used up to 30 times a year by 2030, whereas it has been used just five times a year on average since it

AMAZING FACTS! The Great Stink

Floodwaters don't just ruin your home's carpets and furniture. They can also ruin drinking-water supplies, too. In August 2004, a downpour of rain forced 600,000 tonnes of storm water into London's ageing Victorian drainage system. This in turn forced 50,000 tonnes of raw sewage to spill out into the River Thames, killing thousands of fish and causing a horrible smell to drift across the city. It reminded historians of the 'Great Stink' of 1858 when the smell of untreated sewage in the River Thames forced some people to flee the city. There was even an outbreak of cholera, a deadly disease caused by dirty water. It was this event that led the politicians of the time to say they would build the world's most modern drain system for the city, to prevent it ever happening again. Sadly, over a century later, London's once-modern drains don't appear to be able to cope with a future that will see more flooding due to torrential downpours.

opened in 1983. But the Thames Barrier doesn't protect the city from floodwaters coming down the river. Low-lying cities such as London will now face the twin threat of flooding from the sea and rain-water running down from higher ground further up the river.

London has the money to try to protect itself, but some regions around the world are not so lucky. The ever-increasing risk of flooding in poorer and more vulnerable areas will force millions of people to seek new homes.

HEALTH

A warmer world will introduce new health problems for humans. Perhaps the most dangerous threat will be the increase in water-borne and vector-borne (carried by animals) diseases such as malaria and cholera. Health experts even fear that malaria – a disease transmitted by mosquitoes and currently restricted to much warmer climates – might become established in southerly parts of Britain for up to four months of the year. Elsewhere, as waters rise and flooding increases, animals such as rats and mosquitoes will be able to breed unchecked and prove to be an even greater health risk than they do today. Remember that more than 3,000 children a DAY already die in Africa from malaria.

There is also likely to be an increase in skin cancer across the world as the levels of ultraviolet radiation rise, particularly in countries such as Britain that don't have a population used to dealing with strong sunlight on a regular basis. Warmer weather is also likely to increase the risk of food poisoning, with dairy products and uncooked meat, in particular, 'going off' in the heat much more easily.

Hot, sunny days also aggravate city pollution which can cause breathing problems for many people. On such days, pollution such as car fumes reacts with sunlight to cause smog. Cities such as Los Angeles, Mexico City, São Paulo and Beijing all notoriously suffer from smog. Until the 1950s, London also used to experience terrible smog, before laws were introduced to ban the burning of coal in fireplaces.

Are there any benefits to climate change?

There is certainly one saving grace. Warmer temperatures will lead to fewer cold-related deaths by bringing to a close the age of waking up to find ice on the inside of your window. (Just ask your grandparents.) In Britain, the Department of Health estimates that there are likely to be 20,000 fewer cold-related deaths each winter due to global warming. But the big question is whether this will be cancelled out by the increased number of deaths caused by disasters such as summer heatwaves and extreme floods. Either way, it is nearly always elderly and sick people who suffer from these extremes.

Elsewhere, some farmers might see certain advantages in a warmer climate. The range of crops British farmers can grow might actually increase over the coming decades, meaning we'll have to import less of our food. Get ready to see pepper plants and watermelons growing in a field near you! And as parts of the Mediterranean get too hot to sunbathe, so tourists might start to come to Britain instead of going to, say, Spain to catch some rays. Expect to see Germans, Italians and Swedes fighting for towel space, and not just the usual selection of pasty-looking Brits that line our beaches today!

WILL JELLYFISH RULE THE WORLD?

We can't just ignore the varied effects of climate change. Even if we were mistakenly to think that we'd be fine, many of the animals and plants around us would suffer. Some might be completely wiped out. Would it be right to let that happen?

The reality is that we will, of course, be greatly affected by climate change, and if we are to try to avoid, or at least minimize, the negative impacts – flooding, heatwaves, water shortage, etc. – then we must all urgently find ways to stop pumping so many greenhouse gases into the atmosphere.

5

THE SOLUTIONS

Now, it's time for the fun to begin – learning about how we are going to dig ourselves out of this hole we call climate change! And you'll be pleased to learn that some of the work needed to tackle climate change is already under way – just not yet at the pace that's required.

So, what's the first step?

Well, we need to look at what choices we have before us and to work out which is the best road (or roads) to take. Broadly speaking, we can either **reduce** the amount of pollution we are emitting. Or we can start to **adapt** to our fast-changing world.

But there's also a third option – one that is, ultimately, nearer to what we will collectively end up doing. That's

to say, we will have to both reduce emissions AND learn to adapt to our new climate. In fact, both processes are already under way across the world.

How can we turn off the emissions 'tap'?

In an ideal world, we would stop all pollution from entering the atmosphere – and we would do so by tomorrow. Nearly everyone agrees that we must stop polluting our skies. If we don't, then there is little hope of us ever preventing dangerous climate change.

But to just stop overnight is clearly impossible. After all, could you imagine a world in which we suddenly stopped using our cars or heating our homes? The whole world would come to a grinding halt – and people would get very hungry, cold and grumpy very quickly. And even if we did manage to pull it off, there are still enough greenhouse gases in the atmosphere today to continue to affect our climate for quite a while yet.

No, what we must aim to do now is **minimize** the impacts of climate change by trying not to make the situation any worse than it is already. We must now start to get used to living in a **decarbonized** world, even if, at first, we don't like the thought of it very much. This means we have to reduce our reliance on fossil fuels – oil, coal and gas – by developing other, less polluting sources of energy.

Luckily, there are plenty of other sources of energy besides fuel found underground. There's the sun (the source of all our energy, ultimately!), the wind and the waves. In fact, there is a surprisingly wide range of alternatives to fossil fuels. Each one by itself will probably not be sufficient, but if we use and develop a wide enough mix of alternatives it might help us to say goodbye to fossil fuels once and for all. We can do this, but we just have to be smart and very determined.

Nice one, Sun! Solar power

The sun is our largest source of energy, what's more it's free and it's always 'switched on'! What's not to like? But, to date, we haven't been very wise when it comes to harnessing all this power. Slowly, though, more and more people are realizing that the sun can be used to

heat water and rooms, and to produce electricity, both in their homes and in much larger buildings such as schools and factories. By putting solar panels on the roof, energy from the sun can be captured and put to good use. The best places in the world to use solar panels are, of course, the sunniest and hottest places, such as slap-bang in the middle of the Sahara desert. But even in soggy old Britain, many people are starting to put solar panels on their roofs. At the moment, most people use them to heat up water, but some panels can produce electricity.

And solar energy is not just limited to use in buildings, either. In 2008, a British solar-powered plane took off in Arizona in the USA and stayed in the air for more than three days! During the night, it used batteries that had been charged in the daylight by its solar panels. However, it was extremely small. It weighed just 30kg – about the same as one child!

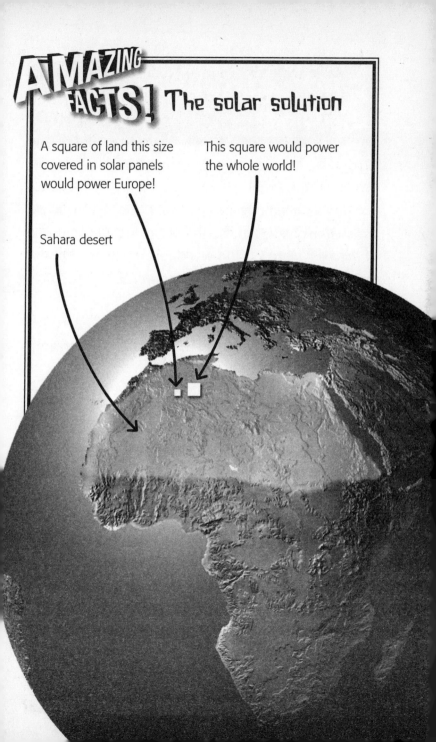

Is the answer blowing in the wind?

Now we're talking. Wind is something Britain knows all about. In fact, we are strong contenders to be the world wind champions. (And, no, I don't mean world fart champions!) Some scientists say that Britain is one of the best places in the world to capture wind power due to the fact that we're so, well, windy.

You have probably seen a giant wind turbine – basically, a big windmill – somewhere before. (They're pretty

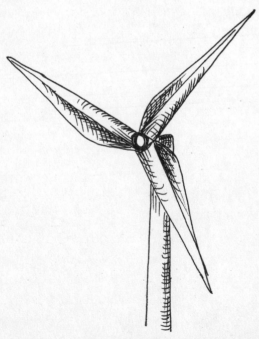

WILL JELLYFISH RULE THE WORLD?

hard to miss!) As the huge blades are pushed around and around by the wind, electricity is produced inside and is then sent along power lines into homes and businesses. When grouped together, some of the largest wind turbines can produce enough electricity to power a whole town or small city.

But not everyone likes them. Some people complain that they are ugly and can cause health problems for those that live close by. And if we were to produce all our power from wind turbines, then we would need to build so many that they would probably need to cover much of the UK, certainly along the western side of the country where most of the strongest winds are found. To get round this problem, some wind turbines are now being built out at sea. But this can also cause problems: sea-birds have been known to fly into the rotating blades.

Wind power will be an important part of our 'energy mix', but is unlikely to be a major contributor. One of its main drawbacks is that, even in Britain, you can't always rely on the wind blowing. What happens on those days when the air is still and calm? You would have to lick your finger and stick it out of the window to see if the wind was blowing before you could watch the television or turn on a light.

THE SOLUTIONS 149

Can you drive a car on chip fat?

Yes – and many people do. You will be able to tell if they do when they drive past you. If the fumes from their car smell like they come from a chip shop then it means that either the car has a tank filled up with the left-over oil used to fry fish and chips, or the driver has just bought some fish and chips and is in a hurry to get home and eat them. In fact, the very first diesel engines invented more than 100 years ago were designed to run on vegetable oil and not the fossil-fuel diesel that is for sale in petrol stations today. And in Brazil, many petrol-engine cars are now powered on ethanol, a fuel made from sugar cane.

What all this shows is that we don't always have to rely on petrol and diesel to power our vehicles. There are alternatives made from plant materials which together are called **biofuels**. They are often described as being **carbon neutral**, which means that, unlike fossil fuels – which release the carbon dioxide into the atmosphere that was previously locked underground for millions of years – they release only the carbon dioxide stored within the plant when it was recently grown.

But there are some big worries about some types of biofuel. Not all of them are as beneficial to the environment as some might have us believe. Biofuels that require intensive farming methods – big tractors, pesticides, etc. – to grow them do end up relying on lots of fossil fuels, albeit indirectly. Worse, some biofuels are grown on land that was previously a rainforest before being chopped down to make way for farming. Is it really sensible to cut down a rainforest to grow fuel for our cars? And what happens when farmers start growing biofuels instead of food for people? People will go hungry and food prices will start to rise. In fact, this has already started to happen.

Therefore, the types of biofuel that offer the best hope to us in tackling climate change are the ones that don't replace food crops or lead to rainforests being cut down. Any biofuel made from our waste is a good idea. This can include the food waste we throw away, or it can include the parts of the food crops that aren't eaten such as the stalks on sugar cane and the chaff from wheat. Some people are also trying to develop biofuels made from algae – that green, slimy stuff you sometimes see floating on lakes or rivers.

How can we wring energy out of water?

Very easily, as it happens, and we've been doing it for ages. Water-wheels have been used for centuries to grind flour and they're a very simple, but effective, use of the fact that water always wants to run downhill. That's why when glaciers melt high up in mountains, the water flows downwards until it joins a river that takes it all the way to the sea.

Dams are used to hold back rivers so that the water can then be forced through giant turbines, producing huge amounts of electricity. Much of Scotland's power is produced this way because it is blessed with lots of deep valleys and raging rivers. Dams produce pollution-free energy, but they do cause environmental problems. By flooding large valleys, dams can damage huge areas of the countryside upstream. Whole towns, forests and farms have to be flooded to make way for the very biggest dams. And the pollution produced when building the dams can also be considerable.

Sea water can be used to generate power, too. Snake-like machines float on the surface and as they twist and rock in the waves their moving 'joints' generate

WILL JELLYFISH RULE THE WORLD?

power. Or a fixed turbine can be placed in a tidal estuary (where a river meets the sea) and as the tide goes in and out, so the water turns the turbine's blades and it produces power. (We can thank the moon for this one as it is responsible for causing our tides to go in and out as it circles the Earth.) There are now plans to build the world's largest such **tidal barrage** across the mouth of the River Severn from southern Wales across to Somerset.

Cardiff

Bristol

There are currently five plans for a Severn Barrage being considered. The most-studied option, shown here, could generate 5% of Britain's energy needs

nuclear power: a big solution with a big problem

The decision whether or not to use nuclear power is perhaps one of the hardest and most controversial questions we now face as we hunt for ways to tackle climate change.

Nuclear power has been around for about half a century, but following some serious accidents – and with a huge question mark over how we dispose of its highly dangerous waste materials – nuclear power has fallen out of favour in recent decades. But now it is back on the table, largely because it produces next to no atmospheric pollution. About 15 per cent of the world's electricity is produced using nuclear power today but some people now want to increase this greatly.

Put very simply, a controlled nuclear reaction is triggered inside a power station and the resulting energy is used to heat water and produce steam, which, in turn, is used to turn the turbines that generate electricity. Most nuclear power stations use a fuel called uranium to trigger the initial reaction. Uranium is first dug out of the ground in places such as Australia and Canada. The big problem with nuclear energy is what to do with

this uranium once it has been used up. Uranium is dangerously radioactive – meaning that it would kill you if you touched it – and it remains this dangerous for thousands of years, so it is hard to know what to do with it. Should it be blasted into space? But what happens if the space rocket carrying it crashed into the ground? Should it be sunk to the very deepest part of the ocean? But what would happen if the container broke open or leaked?

The most likely thing we'll end up doing is bury it far underground. But we still don't seem to be too sure what to do. All we know is that we like the idea of near pollution-free energy. It seems likely that we will have to keep using this technology and hope future generations can work out what to do with the waste. It is a very big risk, but some people feel we now have no choice.

THE SOLUTIONS

Deforestation: or why you should hug a tree

One of the greatest mistakes mankind has made since we first learned to sharpen an axe is cutting down the planet's rainforests. We haven't quite finished the job yet but if we carry on at the current rate, all the rainforests will be almost entirely chopped down by the end of the century. Not only will this have a devastating impact on all the wildlife they contain but it will also make climate change a lot worse.

By **burning** rainforests to make way for farmland, huge amounts of carbon dioxide are released into the atmosphere. In fact, each year about 1.5 billion tonnes of carbon dioxide are released through deforestation – about 20 per cent of all our emissions.

By **destroying** rainforests it means they are no longer around to absorb the carbon dioxide already present in the atmosphere.

These are two highly important reasons not to destroy any more rainforests. It's a very slow process, but people around the world now realize that we all must fight to protect the rainforests.

How a rainforest was saved by kids eating cake

In 1987, during a lesson about the importance of the world's rainforests, a nine-year-old pupil at a small primary school in Sweden stood up in class and asked the teacher how these natural wonders could be saved. The teacher scratched his head. But the children at the school quickly came up with the idea of starting a campaign to raise money so that they could buy up bits of rainforest in order to protect them.

The first thing they did to collect money was to hold a cake sale at their school. With the funds, they bought six hectares of rainforest in the Monteverde preserve in Costa Rica, Central America. News of the campaign soon spread around the world. (In Britain, it even featured on *Blue Peter*.) Children from dozens of countries, including the USA, Germany, Canada, Japan and Britain, joined in and saved up their pocket money to help. Within two years, enough money had been raised to buy 7,000 hectares of rainforest in Costa Rica.

To this day, it is known as the Children's Eternal Rainforest and it will now be protected forever. Furthermore, money continues to be raised and the rainforest has now grown to 22,000 hectares – about half the size of the Isle of Wight. In 1994, enough money was raised to buy up another expanse of rainforest, this time 3,000 hectares in Ecuador, South America.

How many light-bulbs does it take to save a planet?

Switch off the one next to you and I'll tell you the answer. Switching off light-bulbs when we're not using them is just one of the many important ways the world needs to learn how to save energy. If we didn't use up so much energy, we wouldn't need to keep burning so many millions of tonnes of fossil fuels each year.

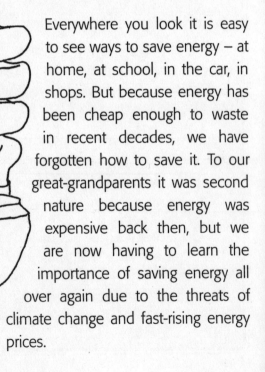

Everywhere you look it is easy to see ways to save energy – at home, at school, in the car, in shops. But because energy has been cheap enough to waste in recent decades, we have forgotten how to save it. To our great-grandparents it was second nature because energy was expensive back then, but we are now having to learn the importance of saving energy all over again due to the threats of climate change and fast-rising energy prices.

WILL JELLYFISH RULE THE WORLD?

At home: hunting down the 'heat leaks'

Can you think of all the different ways we use energy in our homes? When you think about it, there are dozens of ways – heating radiators, heating water, lighting, televisions, radios, fridges, freezers, washing-machines, tumble-driers, hair-driers, telephones, computers . . .

Every single one of these ways of using up energy could be done more efficiently. In fact, scientists and engineers are working hard to try to find ways to build machines and appliances that use less energy. But what about those we already use? Well, we have to try to use them more intelligently by only using them when we absolutely need to, and also by trying to **maximize** their efficiency. This means, say, only using a dishwasher when it is absolutely full, rather than half full. The same can be said of washing-machines. It should also mean not leaving the television on when you go out of the room. Or leaving a mobile charger plugged in when the phone is already fully charged.

Another hugely important way to save energy at home – perhaps the most important of all – is not to waste **heat**. Most of the energy we use at home is needed to heat rooms or water. But most of the heat in our homes escapes through windows, walls and the roof. If you ever climb up into an attic you are likely to see a thick blanket lying on the floor. This is called **insulation** and it is there to try to stop as much heat from escaping from the rooms below as possible. It works in exactly the same way as when you pull a blanket over you at night in bed if you are cold. Warm air wants to rise so it helps to trap it.

Insulation is also wrapped around hot-water tanks to help keep the heat in. And inside many outside walls there is a thin layer of insulation placed between the bricks to help heat escaping this way.

What many people are now realizing is that their homes are not insulated enough. If you have ever felt a strong draught in your home then it means that you could probably find out where the 'heat leak' is located simply by following the draught. Chances are, it will be coming from under the front door or perhaps a rattling window. If you find it, block it up.

ASTOUNDING SCIENCE!

Learn how to grow grass on your head

It's easy. You take a packet of grass seed and sprinkle it on your head. Pour on some water and wait. In just a few weeks you will have a head covered in grass and you will feel a lot warmer for it, too. It's the latest fashion, don't you know?

Oh, perhaps I didn't explain things properly. I didn't mean to say that you should grow grass on your own head. What I meant to say was that some people are now growing grass on top of buildings. **Green roofs**, as they're known, are a brilliant way of increasing the efficiency of a building by using the grass to act just like hair does on your head by trapping the heat. But there's

another big advantage too – green roofs attract lots of wildlife, especially in areas like city centres where there isn't much greenery.

Some schools are starting to place green roofs on their buildings too. And some people don't stop at growing just patches of grass on their roofs – some grow vegetables there, too. You might need to grow one of Jack's Giant Beanstalks to reach it, though!

Transport: or why we need to be trained to use the train

The car is king. No one would argue against this. We love the way a car allows us to get from A to B whenever we want. It means no waiting in the rain for trains or buses.

But cars cause big problems, too. Not only are they responsible for clogging up our roads with traffic, but they are also responsible for about a **quarter** of all our carbon dioxide emissions. Using the car less is one of the most important things we can do to try to tackle climate change. We also need to develop cars that don't guzzle huge amounts of fossil fuels.

The good news is that, as with appliances for the home, scientists and engineers are already busy trying to make cars that use far less fuel than the ones on the road today. This means either they're trying to squeeze more mileage out of the fuel the cars are already using, or they're looking into using alternative sources of fuel

such as electricity, hydrogen and biofuels. One day in the future most of us will probably just charge our cars up at night from a socket in the wall instead of driving to the petrol station to fill the tank.

An even better solution would be if more and more of us stopped using our cars all the time and instead used public transport – buses, trains, trams, tubes, etc. It is a far more efficient use of fuel for one bus to carry 50 people, rather than 50 cars to each carry one person. But many people think public transport is too expensive or too inconvenient when compared to driving their own car. We will have to work hard to change this attitude if we are to tackle climate change. Therefore, one of the most important things governments can do is to ensure that public transport becomes cheaper and more reliable in coming years.

Flying is another form of transport that is highly polluting. In fact, the amount of carbon dioxide released proportionally per person on a return flight to America

The least – and worst – polluting cars on the road

Hats off to Seat who make the **Ibiza Ecomotion**, which the UK government recognizes as the least-polluting car on the road. It produces just 99 grams of carbon dioxide for every kilometre that it travels.

This is more than five times cleaner than the most-polluting car on the market – the **Lamborghini Diablo Roadster**, which produces – cough, spplIarggh, choke, cough – 520 grams of carbon dioxide for every kilometre that it travels.

The average family car in the UK emits about 180 grams of CO_2 per kilometre travelled, although politicians across Europe want this to drop down to 120 grams over the next few years.

VCAcarfueldata.org.uk, 2008

is the same as would be emitted by heating your home throughout the whole of the winter. Here, however, alternatives are harder to find. After all, when did you last hear of anyone swimming to America for their holidays? But we will have to fly less and try to choose alternatives when we can, such as catching the train into Europe instead of always getting a flight.

Food: thinking with your stomach

Wait a moment! Don't put that snack in your mouth quite yet. Did you know that when you eat any food you are also causing pollution? Of course, I'm not proposing that none of us ever eat again, but there are some important things to consider when choosing what to eat. In fact, thinking about food – something I do quite a lot of – is one of the most important ways we can do our bit to tackle climate change.

Let's take a meal most of us like to eat – a roast dinner. Think of all the different things on the plate. There's the roast meat, of course. Then there are the roast potatoes. And on the side you might have peas, carrots and perhaps some cabbage. Oh, and some gravy.

There's a story behind every one of those foods. For example, who grew the peas? Where did they travel from? Britain, or did they come by aeroplane from far away? Where were the cows reared that provided the beef? How was the cabbage grown? And how was the food packaged? Did you have to drive to get the food from the supermarket, or did you grow any of it yourself?

Eating meat – a chewy dilemma

Many of us eat meat and really enjoy it. But not everyone eats it – some think that it is cruel to eat an animal, or it is forbidden as part of their religion. These people are known as **vegetarians**. Some people go further and choose not to eat anything that contains animal products, such as milk, cheese and eggs. These people are known as **vegans**. And I bet you didn't know that there are some people who don't eat fruit or vegetables that were picked when they were 'alive'. Instead, they wait until the food drops from the plant, such as when apples fall off trees. These people are called **fruitarians** – although their numbers are very few.

But there's a new reason not to eat meat – or not to eat so much of it, anyway. The reason is the high carbon footprint of many meats, particularly beef. Scientists in Japan calculated in 2007 that producing a kilogram of beef – about what a family might expect to eat during a roast dinner – generates as much pollution as driving a car non-stop for three hours. This is because cows emit lots of methane when they burp and fart. Another important factor is how much energy is required to feed the cows. Many of them don't just eat grass – they also get fed specially produced animal feed, particularly during the winter

WILL JELLYFISH RULE THE WORLD?

when they are kept indoors for much of the time.

Chicken, lamb and pork have a smaller carbon footprint by comparison, but it is still worth trying to reduce the amount of meat you eat – not just for your own health, but for the health of the planet too.

During the First and Second World Wars, meat and other foods were **rationed**, which means people were only allowed to eat a certain amount of these foods every week because there was little to go around. Some people now argue that some meats and animal products should again be rationed so that we can try to reduce our carbon emissions.

Here's what one person's rations were during the Second World War for a whole week. Do you think you could live on this?

- **Bacon and ham:** 4oz (100g)
- **Meat:** to the value of 1s. 2d. (one shilling and 'tuppence' – two pence), which typically bought you about 1lb 3oz (540 g). Sausages were rationed only from 1942 to 1944, but were always hard to find
- **Cheese:** 1oz (28g) – vegetarians were allowed 3oz (85g) of extra cheese, by giving up their meat ration
- **Margarine:** 4oz (100g)
- **Butter:** 2oz (50g)
- **Milk:** 3 pints (1.8 litres)
- **Eggs:** 1 fresh egg. Or 1 packet of dried egg (equivalent to 12 fresh eggs) every four weeks

All of these stories help to determine the **carbon footprint** of your food – in other words, how much carbon dioxide is emitted into the atmosphere as a result of the way the food is grown, processed, refrigerated, packaged and transported. The carbon footprint of your food can also be affected by the way it is cooked. For example, a roast dinner needs a long time in the oven to cook, which uses up lots of energy.

It is now the job of both those who eat food – er, that's all of us – and those who produce and sell it to make sure we try to reduce the impact of food's carbon footprint.

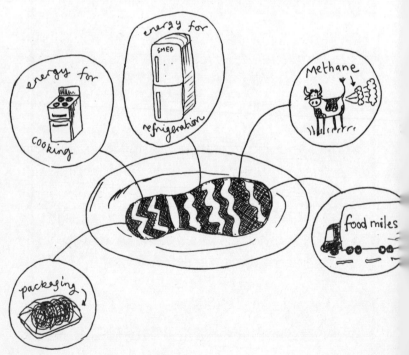

Changing the world: how do you drive a donkey – with a carrot or a stick?

How do you convince everyone in the world to change the way they lead their lives? It's a question that now troubles many of the world's politicians and leaders. Do you tell them what to do and punish them if they don't do it? Or do you help them to make the changes by making these the cheapest and easiest options available?

People often refer to this as 'the carrot or the stick', meaning that if you had a stubborn donkey who refused to move forward, would you dangle a carrot in front of its nose to tease it forward, or would you hit it gently with a stick instead?

Most people think a combination of both is the right way to persuade people – a mixture of rewards and punishments. What would make you tidy up your room? The threat of being grounded for a week if you didn't, or the prospect of being allowed to watch your favourite programme each day if you did?

One of the main ways governments around the world are now trying to stop carbon emissions from rising any further is by introducing a limit – known as a **cap** – on all the big polluting companies. Each company is given a certain number of permits that allow them to cause a fixed amount of pollution each year. If they go over this amount they must buy extra permits from another company that has permits to spare because they've managed to keep beneath their limit. This is a good example of the 'carrot and stick' in action. The company that over-polluted has been punished by having to spend money buying extra permits; whereas the company that under-polluted is rewarded by being paid for its spare ones. Governments hope this system will persuade companies to pollute less and less each year. They do this by lowering the cap each year, too.

The first important step towards introducing this system came on 11 December 1997 when politicians from all over the world met up in the Japanese city of Kyoto to sign what is now known as the **Kyoto Protocol**. The initial promise was that countries who signed up to it would, between 2008 and 2012, try to reduce their greenhouse-gas emissions by 5 per cent compared to levels in 1990.

To date, there has been mixed success. Some countries have done well, some not so well. And some countries, such as America, haven't even agreed to take part in the scheme! But some argue that at least it's a start and that when politicians meet again to agree what the caps should be after 2012, then there will be a much stronger commitment and determination by many more countries to reduce emissions.

Sometimes – with or without the carrot or stick to guide them – you have to trust and hope the donkeys are travelling in the right direction.

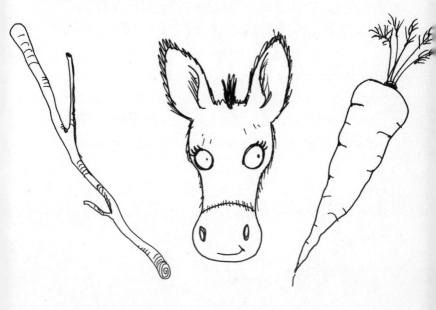

6

WHAT CAN I DO TO HELP?

The planet certainly needs all the help it can get! If each and every one of the six and a half billion people on Earth – including you – pitches in and tries to do their bit, then we've got a great chance of preventing many of the scariest consequences of climate change.

But where to begin? Turn over the page to find out . . .

BEFORE YOU GET STARTED ...

You can always learn more about climate change by using the Internet. Here are some good starting points ...

news.bbc.co.uk/cbbcnews/hi/specials/climate_change

www.newscientist.com/topic/climate-change

But a word of caution: always be careful when you're online. Never give out any kind of personal information – like your name, address, or the name of your school. And never, ever set up a meeting with someone you meet online.

www.epa.gov/climatechange/kids/

peopleandplanet.org/

www.metoffice.gov.uk/climatechange/guide/keyfacts/

When you're looking at websites, remember that not everything you read will be true. Take in all the info with a pinch of salt. There are lots of people creating websites out there, and some of the information can be exactly that: created. Before you go online, get permission from a parent or another adult in your home. Better still, look around the websites together.

WILL JELLYFISH RULE THE WORLD?

What you can do at school

CHALLENGE RIVAL SCHOOLS IN YOUR AREA TO A 'CLIMATE BATTLE'

Work out how much energy each school uses up in a year. (Ask the head teachers to look at the energy bills.) Let's say it's 100,000 kilowatt-hours of electricity a year. Now divide this total by the number of pupils in the school. Let's say it's 100. That means the school uses 1,000 kilowatt-hours of energy per pupil per year. Make a league table of results along with the other schools

and then hail the winner. Now set a target for next year and let the Climate Battles commence! Bragging rights are at stake.

INVITE A SPEAKER TO YOUR SCHOOL

Form a Climate Committee at your school – it could just be a handful of friends concerned about climate change. Together try to think of someone you could invite to your school to talk about climate change at assembly. It could be a scientist from a local university or college. It could be a local MP. It could be a wildlife expert. Perhaps someone you know has a parent whose job might be affected by climate change – say, a farmer?

HOLD AN 'AUCTION OF GREEN PROMISES'

This is a fun way to raise money for school funds AND get people to do something to help prevent climate change. For example, try to persuade a parent to pledge to take public transport to work for a week rather than use the car. Or pledge that you will go meat-free for a week.

HOLD A 'GREEN FAIR'

Many schools around the country are installing solar panels on their roofs, but these can cost thousands of pounds to buy. So why not organize 'Green Fairs' at the schools to help raise the money needed?

TAKE THE SCHOOL'S TEMPERATURE

Your school is sick. It's feeling too hot. It needs its temperature taken. Find a thermometer (ask a science teacher) and then record the temperature in every room and corridor in the school. Classrooms need only be heated to 18°C, whereas gyms and corridors can be even cooler at just 15°C. Any warmer than this and the school is wasting energy unnecessarily. Present your findings to the head teacher and tell them that you've just worked out how they can save money and the climate at the same time!

ORGANIZE A SCHOOL VISIT TO A WIND TURBINE

Ask your teachers if the school visit this term can be centred around climate change. You could visit a local wind turbine, perhaps? Or you could visit a home that uses solar power?

WRITE A LETTER TO YOUR LOCAL MP

Demand from them that, as your area's representative, they take more action on climate change. Get everyone in the school to sign the letter. It's important to let MPs know in writing if you are not happy with the decisions they take in Parliament and that you all passionately care about this issue. After all, one day their jobs will depend on your votes.

VOTE FOR A LOCAL 'GREEN HERO'

Draw up a shortlist of people in your area that have done something good for the environment. It could be a street sweeper, or it could be a parent who always walks their children to school. Now ask the head teacher if the school can recognize their achievements with a special prize, as chosen by the pupils.

WILL JELLYFISH RULE THE WORLD?

BECOME A 'CARBON DETECTIVE'

Someone at your school needs to be responsible for checking that the building is as energy-efficient as it can possibly be. Your school needs an energy champion – someone who checks for draughts, who makes sure that rooms are not overheated, and who watches out for open doors and windows during the winter. Maybe this responsibility should be given to a prefect if you have one? Or perhaps this important person should be nominated each term by all the pupils in the school, or in each year?

For more information about how the Government is trying to establish 'carbon detectives' at every school, visit **www.carbondetectives.org.uk**

BECOME A POLITICIAN

OK, I know you're a bit young – you need to be 21 to become a Member of Parliament – but you could join the Youth Parliament. There are around 500 MYPs (Members of the Youth Parliament) around the country, aged 11–18. There's one MYP for each Local Education Authority in the country. Why not try to get elected yourself and then you can shout even louder about climate change? For more information, visit **www.ukyouthparliament.org.uk**

START A WALKING BUS

It's a really great idea that's catching on all over the country. Instead of everyone being driven to school in their parents' cars, some children are now walking to school together in a long line known as a Walking Bus. Parents take it in turn throughout the week supervising the 'bus' as it makes its way to school, picking up pupils from their homes as it moves along. It's safe, good for the environment and helps everyone get fit. For more information, visit **www.dft.gov.uk/pgr/sustainable/schooltravel/grantsforwalkingbuses/howtosetupawalkingbus**

SHARE A LIFT

If starting a Walking Bus is not possible – it is only really suited to schools in towns and cities where people live close to the school – then try to start up a lift-share scheme. Rather than having each pupil brought to school in their own car, why not see if parents can take it in turns picking up other pupils too? It saves fuel, reduces school-gate traffic and makes the parents' lives easier. Another triple whammy!

The incredible story of William 'Windmill' Kamkwamba

When William in Malawi, a small land-locked country in south-east Africa, was 14 years old his parents said that they couldn't afford to send him to his village school any more. However, William was a very determined boy and decided to continue his education by teaching himself! He walked to the nearest library and borrowed some books. One was called *Using Energy*. Inside he saw a picture of a windmill and decided that he would try to build one for himself at home.

He looked around his village for anything that he could use – wooden poles, broken pipes, old shoes, copper wires, his father's old bicycle – and started to build his windmill.

At first it was a hobby, but he soon realized that if he could build a windmill that could produce electricity he might be able to solve a really big problem. One of his younger sisters – he was one of seven children – had developed a nasty cough because the family used smoky paraffin candles at night because there was no electricity in the village.

WILL JELLYFISH RULE THE WORLD?

William had the brilliant idea of using a small windmill to generate enough electricity to power a light-bulb. Within a few weeks it was up and running, and his sister's cough soon cleared up. He became a hero in his village!

Word spread and it wasn't long before newspapers in Malawi heard about his remarkable windmill and wrote about it. His story soon spread even further and he was invited to America to talk about his windmill in front of business leaders. He now has fans all over the world. Better still, he returned home and improved his windmill. It was soon powerful enough to provide lighting for his whole home as well as power two radios and a mobile-phone charger! His inspiring story and ingenuity earned him a place at one of Africa's most prestigious schools, in South Africa.

William has shown us all that everyone, no matter what their background or circumstances, can really make a difference.

You can learn more about William at his blog: **www. williamkamkwamba. typepad.com**

GIVE YOUR HOME AN ENERGY EXAM

Sit up straight. Pencils at the ready. OK, you may start. It's time to test your home on how much energy it wastes. Ask if you can see the home's energy bills. You can now start to plot a graph to see how much energy the home uses in a whole year. Over time you will probably

notice that during the winter you use far more energy than in the summer. This is because of all the heat that must be generated. Now see where energy and heat are being wasted around the home – e.g. draughts, left-on appliances, old-fashioned light-bulbs. Draw a plan of the whole house, pointing out all the places where you have located waste. Now hand it to your parents or guardian and tell them that you've pinpointed all the places where the house is wasting energy and money. You have just performed a vital task – the average home in the UK produces just over 6 tonnes of CO_2 per year, and helping to achieve any reduction to this total is very important.

ISSUE A FLOOD WARNING

Climate change is predicted to increase the risk of flooding in certain areas of the country. Check to see if your home could be at risk of flooding. You can type in your postcode at **www.environment-agency.gov.uk/ homeandleisure/floods/31656.aspx/**

WATCH OUT FOR PHANTOM POWER

Be afraid, be very afraid. There are appliances in your home that are using up electricity even when they are switched off. Energy experts call this 'phantom power' or 'vampire power'. The guilty appliances are things such as mobile-phone chargers and digital-camera chargers that

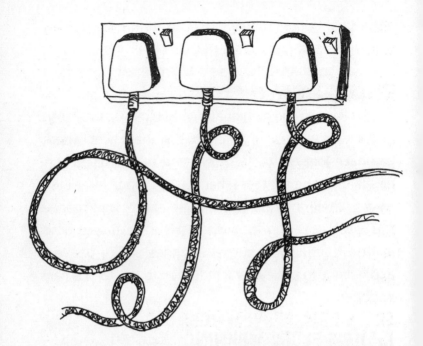

use small amounts of power even when the appliance is not plugged into the charger. Computer consoles can also be responsible. To prevent this, either pull the charger out of the socket, or switch the socket off.

STAMP OUT STAND-BY

Appliances that use remote controls – TVs, DVD players, set-top boxes, radios, etc. – all tend to have a stand-by facility. This means you can 'turn off' the appliance from your armchair without having to actually get up and turn it off properly. But the trouble with stand-by buttons is that they use power even when everyone is asleep at

WILL JELLYFISH RULE THE WORLD?

night. It is far better to make sure all appliances are switched off properly when they're not in use.

STICK ON THE KETTLE . . .

. . . but make sure it is not too full. Heating water is one of the most energy-intensive activities you can do in the home, so it's really important to heat up only what you need. If you need just one cup of tea, only place one cupful of water in the kettle. Better still, fill a thermos flask with hot water in the morning so that you don't need to boil cold water from scratch throughout the day.

EAT A LOW-CARBON MEAL

What's this, you're thinking? Toast that is not burnt? Not quite. A low-carbon meal is one in which you've thought about all the ingredients to see if they have the smallest carbon footprint possible. Probably the lowest-carbon meal you could have would be one in which all the ingredients were grown at home – no tractors, no supermarkets, no packaging, no trucks. But this isn't really a possibility for most people. Probably the most important consideration you can realistically make when thinking about low-carbon eating is the cooking method you choose. There's a big difference in energy use between baking a potato for an hour in an oven heated to 200°C and, say, cubed, peeled potatoes boiled or steamed in water for 10 minutes. Microwaving the potatoes would use even less energy (but might not be so tasty!). Visit **www.eatlowcarbon. org** and have some fun calculating the different carbon impacts of your favourite meals and foods. You'll soon see how carbon-intensive meat and dairy products can be, for example. Oh, and try to drink tap water rather than drinking bottled water. Shipping water across the country (and the world, in some cases!) requires huge amounts of energy, in addition to using up lots of plastic and glass for the bottles.

CHANGE A LIGHT-BULB

About 95 per cent of the energy used by old-style light-bulbs (properly known as **incandescent** light-bulbs) produces heat rather than light. What a waste! Ask if the light-bulbs in your home can be swapped for CFLs (compact fluorescent lamps), as they use just a fifth of their energy as heat.

DRAW YOUR CURTAINS

To save as much heat as possible when it's cold, it makes a big difference if all the curtains in the home are drawn as soon as the sun goes down. They act like blankets around your windows. Otherwise lots of heat will escape through the glass. But remember to open them again in the morning!

HANG UP YOUR CLOTHES

OK, you've probably heard this before. Children suffer messy-room syndrome all over the world. But this is different. This refers to when clothes are drying after coming out of the washing-machine all wet. Drying clothes on a washing-line, be it outdoors or indoors, prevents a considerable amount of energy being used to dry them in a tumble-drier.

SHOWER YOURSELF IN GLORY

Taking a shower rather than running a bath saves both water and energy because you use far less hot water – unless the shower is a power shower. Power showers can use more hot water than a bath, so check first.

SHUT THAT DOOR!

It's really important never to leave the door of your fridge or freezer open longer than absolutely necessary. Due to the fact that they are switched on 24 hours a day, 365 days a year, fridges and freezers use more power than any other appliance in your home. So no hanging on an open fridge door wondering what you'd like to eat next!

FLUSHED WITH SUCCESS

Every time you flush the loo 6–12 litres of drinking water disappear down the hole into the sewers. Water will get increasingly precious and scarce as climate change advances, so it makes sense to treat it as a limited and precious resource **now**. There is an old saying: 'If it's brown, flush it down; if it's yellow, let it mellow.' In other words, if all you've had is a pee, perhaps consider not flushing until the next time you visit the loo. You might want to talk this over with the other people sharing your home first, though!

BE A WOOLLY MAMMOTH

Rather than asking for the heating to be switched on or up when you feel a chill, put on an extra layer. It doesn't take any energy at all to pull on a jumper – whereas to heat up the whole of your home will burn up lots of extra energy.

REDUCE, REUSE, RECYCLE

You are probably already the best recycler in your home. If so, give yourself a big pat on the back. But recycling is actually the **last** course of action you should take when trying to reduce waste. The first priority is to reduce the amount of 'stuff' that you ask for, or buy, in the first place. How much of it do you really **need**? And before you throw anything away, or put it out for recycling, is there any other use for it? Or, if broken, can it be repaired?

MAKE A CLIMATE-FRIENDLY GARDEN

With seasons shifting and the climate becoming ever more erratic with droughts and flooding, it is important to help any wildlife visiting a garden as much as possible. If you're lucky enough to have a garden or balcony, providing food, water and shelter are probably your most important tasks. Birds, bees, reptiles, insects and mammals can all do with your help. Here's just a few things you can try . . .

- Install a water-butt to collect rain-water
- Build a feeding table for birds
- Build a bird-box for a family of birds to nest in
- Build a compost heap, or wormery, to reduce the waste you throw out and to improve the quality of your soil
- Sow some wildflower seeds on your lawn – they will attract insects and birds, and reduce the amount of mowing
- Grow some vegetables. Begin with some tomatoes – they will even grow in a small pot on a window-sill (see page 201)

WILL JELLYFISH RULE THE WORLD?

Plant a tree. It could be an apple tree, an oak, or even just some willows to make a new hedge, but each one will be among the most important things you will ever do in a garden. Trees shelter and provide food for animals. Trees absorb carbon dioxide from the atmosphere. And trees improve and secure the soil underneath them

FREE HOUSE!

AVAILABLE NOW FOR BIRD FAMILY!

What you can do with your friends and family

INTERVIEW THE OLDEST MEMBER OF YOUR FAMILY

Ask them what the weather used to be like when they were a child. Have they noticed weather patterns and seasons change over the course of their lifetime? Write down what they tell you so you can create a record of this important information.

CHOOSE A HOLIDAY

The choice your family makes about where you all go on holiday could be among the most important decisions you make all year in terms of its climate-change impact. Just one person flying from, say, Britain to Florida is responsible for the same level of emissions as one car over the course of an entire year. So if there are four people in your family and you all go to Florida on holiday, the total emissions will represent a huge chunk of the pollution you are all responsible for over the whole year. Why not suggest that you holiday closer to home this year? What about the perfect low-carbon holiday – camping?

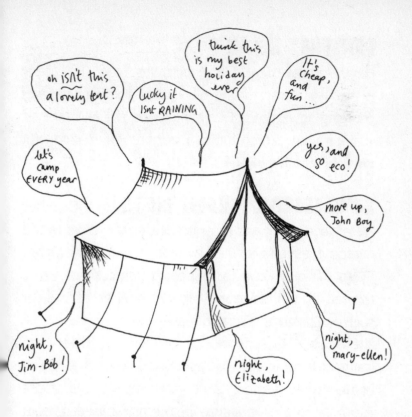

DRIVEN TO DISTRACTION

Drive your parents potty by constantly telling them to remember that their driving style can have a big influence on how much fuel their car uses over an entire year. For example, accelerating and braking hard will increase the **fuel burn**. Also, smooth but quick gear changes can improve the fuel efficiency of a car. To reduce fuel burn further, keep the windows wound up tight, keep the car clutter-free to reduce weight, and keep the tyres pumped up to the correct pressure.

DON THAT HELMET

Have you taken your Bikeability test yet? (Bikeability is the new name for the old **cycling proficiency test**.) Learning how to cycle with confidence, skill and safety is vital for a low-carbon future. For more information, visit **www.bikeability.org.uk**

COME BEARING 'GREEN' GIFTS

We all love giving and receiving presents, but we can all overdo it, especially when it comes to wrapping paper! Try to think of ways to reduce the amount of waste created by birthdays and other special times of year, such as Christmas. Can you make your own cards? What about using newspaper or saved wrapping paper from last year to wrap your presents? And rather than giving someone some more 'stuff' as a present, what about giving them an experience or memory-based present instead, such as a collection of favourite photographs from the past year?

INVITE A FRIEND TO BE YOUR 'CARBON BUDDY'

Why not see if a friend would like to join you in the challenge of trying to find as many ways to save energy in your lives as possible? Both of you write a list and see who comes up with the most.

WILL JELLYFISH RULE THE WORLD?

PUT ON YOUR LAB COAT, PROFESSOR CARBON
It's time to conduct some experiments . . .

Keep a carbon diary: Every day, write down all the ways that you think you used up energy – travelling to school, cooking your food, heating your home, etc. Plot a graph and see if you can reduce the total week by week.

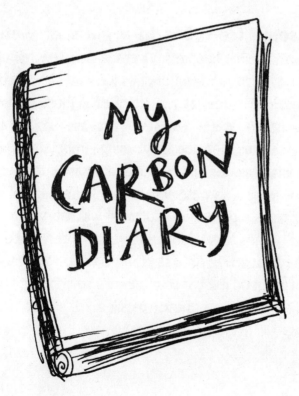

Keep a weather diary: Next to your energy use, write down your observations about the weather. Ideally, set up a small weather station at school, or even at home if possible. This will allow you to keep a record of the temperature, rainfall and air pressure. Over time you will be able to see the seasonal changes. One of the most important things you can do is make a record in spring of when you see certain things – bees, sorts of flower, etc. – for the first time.

Put some ice-cubes in a glass of water: Now watch what happens. Over the next few minutes the ice will start to melt. But does the water level rise in the glass? No, it doesn't. Now think of all those icebergs in the ocean. Water levels will not rise around the world if they all melt due to warming temperatures. But watch what happens if you put another ice-cube in the glass of water. The water will spill over the edge of the glass. This is representative of what will happen to the world's oceans if water that is currently frozen as ice on landmasses such as Antarctica and Greenland begins to melt. It's a good illustration of why it's so important that we all try to prevent these so-called 'ice sheets' from melting.

Build a mini-greenhouse: Take a big plastic bottle and cut it in half. (Carefully! Ask for help, if necessary.) Now take two small garden plant pots and fill them with earth or compost. Plant a tomato seed in both pots and water them. Now place a plastic bottle half over one of the pots. Place both pots on a window-sill – and wait. You should see the seed in the pot with the plastic cover germinate and grow first. This is because the plastic cover is trapping the heat and moisture inside, helping to provide the perfect conditions for growing tomatoes. In a way, you have replicated the Greenhouse Effect that keeps the surface of Planet Earth warm. But on a hot day there is a danger you could kill your tomato plant if you leave the plastic cover on it, because it will overheat. This is the problem when the Greenhouse Effect prevents heat from escaping. It will build up and there is an ever-growing risk that this heat will begin to threaten life.

CONCLUSION

How are you feeling now that you've finished reading this book? Surprised? Angry? Sad? Frustrated? Or are you feeling invigorated? Motivated? Hopeful? Optimistic? Probably a little bit of all of these things, if you're anything like me. I think we can all agree that climate change *is* a real worry. But we humans have a good track record of solving problems and facing up to difficult challenges.

Each and every person on this planet – including, and most importantly, you – can now be part of the solution. All of us have a choice: either we choose to ignore the warning signs or we fight as hard as we can by changing our lifestyles now to avoid the perils climate change could bring. It's not really a difficult choice to make when you think about it, is it?

In fact, 'change' is the most important word to be found anywhere in this book. As Mahatma Gandhi, the inspiring Indian leader, once said: 'You must be the change you wish to see in the world.'

EXTRA STUFF

A brief history of Earth

4.6 billion years ago Planet Earth is formed out of the debris of a huge galactic explosion called a supernova. It is a desolate place without an atmosphere and is constantly being bombarded by rocks from space. This era is called the Hadean Period by geologists, after Hades (the name the Ancient Greeks gave to Hell). The universe, which was created by the 'Big Bang', is already 9.1 billion years old at this point.

4 billion years ago The first life appears on Earth, but it's nothing more than tiny single-cell organisms called **prokaryotes**. No one knows for sure how or why life began at this moment.

3.8 billion years ago The Archean Period begins. The planet is a mass of erupting volcanoes and flowing lava. It is boiling hot and stinks of noxious gases such as sulphur and methane.

3.3 billion years ago The first supercontinent, or giant landmass, is formed – called Vaalbara – but it breaks up 500 million years later.

4.6 BILLION

4 BILLION

3.8 BILLION

3.3 BILLION

WILL JELLYFISH RULE THE WORLD?

2.5 BILLION

2.5 billion years ago The first oxygen appears in the atmosphere when bacteria begin to convert the light from the sun into this life-giving element – a process we now call **photosynthesis**. It leads to the 'Oxygen Catastrophe', whereby the excess oxygen kills off most of the bacteria. However, some survive and new, more advanced life-forms are born in the new atmosphere.

1 BILLION

1 billion years ago Multi-celled animals and plants start to appear.

790 MILLION

790 million years ago The Earth experiences a period of repeated glaciations – whereby much of the planet freezes over and is covered in ice. Some scientists call this period 'Snowball Earth'.

542 MILLION

542 million years ago The Cambrian Period begins. The very first insects, spiders and crabs appear.

359 MILLION

359 million years ago The Carboniferous Period begins – a warm, tropical period in which most of the dead animal and plant life that we now know as oil and coal was buried under the ground.

250 million years ago The Triassic Period begins. The first flowering plants and flying creatures known as pterosaurs appear. A huge supercontinent called Pangea forms around the equator – it includes all the landmasses we know today as Australia, the Americas, Africa and Eurasia. Pangea is a very hot and dry place. The first dinosaurs appear.

250 MILLION

200 million years ago The Jurassic Period begins – the age of the dinosaurs. Pangea begins to break up into small continents. Large reptiles are the dominant life-form on the planet.

200 MILLION

145 million years ago The Cretaceous Period begins. The climate cools and becomes wetter – snow begins to fall at the polar regions – before heating up again.

145 MILLION

68 million years ago The *Tyrannosaurus rex* rules the world!

68 MILLION

WILL JELLYFISH RULE THE WORLD?

65.5 MILLION

65.5 million years ago A mass extinction occurs across the whole planet, killing off the dinosaurs and many other life-forms. Scientists suspect that a giant asteroid hit the Earth where the Caribbean Sea is today and caused a huge explosion that sent billions of tonnes of ash into the air, blocking out the sun and leading to a deep winter that lasted many years. This event marks the start of the Palaeogene Period.

55.8 MILLION

55.8 million years ago The Earth experiences another mass extinction event in which average global temperatures rise by 6°C in just 20,000 years. Scientists are still unsure exactly why this event occurred, but they suspect that something – perhaps a comet strike – triggered a vast release of methane from the sea-bed. Many species die out completely, but the new era sees the arrival of the first mammals, which thrive in the balmy atmosphere. Forests begin to grow on the land, reaching from pole to pole.

33.9 million years ago The continents are slowly starting to move towards their current positions. Antarctica, for example, is drifting alone towards the South Pole and is starting to develop an ice covering. The Alps mountain range in Europe is starting to be formed.

33.9 MILLION

27.5 million years ago The largest-known volcanic eruption occurs in what is now Colorado, USA. Five thousand cubic kilometres of ash and lava pour out of the La Garita volcano.

27.5 MILLION

23 million years ago The Neogene Period begins. Compared to most other classes of animals, mammals and birds continue to evolve at speed.

23 MILLION

18 million years ago The first modern sharks appear in the oceans, including the giant meglodon which is up to 18 metres long. It feeds on whales with its massive teeth that measure 18cm in length.

18 MILLION

5 million years ago North and South America come together.

5 MILLION

WILL JELLYFISH RULE THE WORLD?

2.2 MILLION

2.2 million years ago The first humanoid animals – *Homo habilis* – appear in Africa. Their brains are half the size of ours and they cannot stand upright, but they start to use stones as tools – the Stone Age has begun.

1.8 MILLION

1.8 million years ago The Pleistocene Period begins, marked by repeated ice ages.

700,000

700,000 years ago *Homo erectus* – the first humanoids to stand up on their back legs – learn how to use fire.

250,000

250,000 years ago The first woolly mammoths appear as the ice ages continue.

200,000

200,000 years ago The first modern humans – *Homo sapiens* – begin to appear. The rest, as they say, is history. Well, our history anyway – farming, writing, Bronze Age, Iron Age, the Egyptians, the Greeks, the Romans, Buddha, Jesus, Muhammad, the first printed book, the Industrial Revolution, electricity, cars, World Wars, television, pop music, space exploration, home computers . . .

Clever climatologists

It has taken almost two centuries for scientists to agree that humans are causing climate change and there have been many landmarks of discovery along the way . . .

1825 **Joseph Fourier**, a French mathematician and physicist, proposes the idea that the Earth would be much colder if it didn't have an atmosphere. Fourier is now widely credited with having 'discovered' the Greenhouse Effect.

1865 **John Tyndall**, an Irish physicist and mountaineer, shows that carbon dioxide, water vapour and other greenhouse gases do, indeed, absorb heat in the atmosphere and act together to help dictate air temperature. He also suggests that variations to the amounts of these gases in the atmosphere could cause the climate to change.

1896 **Svante Arrhenius**, a Swedish chemist and Nobel Prize-winner, proves that changes to levels of carbon dioxide in the atmosphere can alter the Earth's surface temperature. He calculates that halving CO_2 levels in the atmosphere would

WILL JELLYFISH RULE THE WORLD?

result in a temperature drop of 4–5°C, whereas doubling them would increase the temperature by 5–6°C. He also develops a theory about why Earth has experienced ice ages and believes that a rise in temperature would be a good thing for humans as it would prevent another ice age. You can't really blame him!

1897 **Thomas Chrowder Chamberlin**, an American geologist, develops a detailed theory about why the climate on Earth has repeatedly changed throughout its history. His theory includes not just the influence of greenhouse gases in the atmosphere, but also the influences of the oceans and volcanoes too. He describes how climatic cycles such as ice ages can be maintained through 'feedbacks' – a repeating loop whereby carbon dioxide becomes absorbed into the ground and rocks, then released back into the atmosphere. He also challenges the belief by Lord Kelvin, a prominent Scottish physicist and engineer, that the Earth is only 100 million years old, saying instead that it is much, much older. (It wasn't the last time Lord Kelvin was proved spectacularly wrong on something – in 1895 he said that 'heavier-than-air flying machines are impossible'. Just eight years later the Wright Brothers made the first-ever powered flight by humans at Kitty Hawk in North Carolina. Oops!)

1935 Weather observers in the USA notice that temperatures are slightly higher than when records first began in the 19th century. Widespread media reports begin to discuss whether the world is warming up. It's also at this time that **Milutin Milankovi**, a Serbian mathematician and engineer, develops his theory about how the tilt of the Earth's axis, in combination with slight 'wobbles' in the Earth's orbit around the sun, can affect the climate and cause ice ages. His theory is now popularly known as the **Milankovitch Cycles**.

1938 **Guy Callendar**, an English engineer and amateur scientist, publishes a scientific paper arguing that the carbon dioxide emitted from the burning of fossil fuels by humans is having an impact on the Earth's atmosphere. He notices that there had been a rise in global temperatures during the early 20th century that corresponded with a rise in levels of carbon dioxide in the atmosphere since the beginning of the Industrial Revolution. Like Arrhenius before him, Callendar argues that a rise in global temperatures would be good news for humans because it would delay a 'return of the deadly glaciers'. During the Second World War he helps to design a way of clearing fog from runways so that bombers can land safely. But because he was seen as an 'amateur', his climate change theories were widely discredited or ignored by other scientists until the 1960s.

1956 **Norman Phillips** produces what is now considered to be the first-ever computer model used to predict the weather and longer-term climatic trends. But due to a common error with the earlier computers of that period, when it tries to predict the weather for a month ahead it blows up! He was later to become the principal scientist at the National Weather Service at America's National Meteorological Center.

1958 **Charles David Keeling** begins recording atmospheric carbon dioxide levels at the 3km-high Mauna Loa Observatory in Hawaii and at the South Pole. Over the coming years his findings show how carbon dioxide levels are on the rise. Although a funding freeze in the 1960s means that he has to abandon his efforts at the South Pole, his measurements at Mauna Loa continue right up until his death in 2005 – and still continue today. In 1958, he found that there were 315 parts per million by volume (ppmv) of carbon dioxide in the atmosphere. This had risen to 385 ppmv by 2008 – a 22 per cent increase in just 50 years. This steady rise in CO_2 levels is now widely referred to as the 'Keeling Curve' in his honour.

1964 **Willi Dansgaard**, a Danish palaeo-climatologist (someone who studies the Earth's past climates), travels to Greenland to examine samples of ice that have been drilled out from 1.5km below the surface by the US army. He realizes that by studying the air bubbles frozen within the ice he can find out what the atmosphere was like on Earth up to 100,000 years ago when the very deepest bubbles were first trapped. Later studies of the ice cores show that there seemed to be warmer periods between ice ages that tended to last about 10,000 years. Because the 'interglacial' warming period the world is currently experiencing is already about 10,000 years old, scientists come to the conclusion in the early 1970s that the world is imminently heading for another ice age. It triggers lots of headlines around the world about 'global **cooling**'!

1968 **John Mercer**, an American glaciologist, argues that the West Antarctic Ice Sheet, a large portion of the Antarctic landmass separated from the rest of the continent by a huge mountain range, could melt and collapse into the sea if atmospheric temperatures were to rise even slightly. His views were widely ignored at the time, but climatologists today now believe that he was largely correct. Should this event happen, sea levels around the world could rise by about five metres, flooding many of the world's leading cities such as London and New York.

1970 Following the successful landing of men on the moon in 1969 by America's National Aeronautics and Space Administration, otherwise known as **NASA**, climate scientists go to the US government and argue that the world urgently needs a 'wet NASA'. The National Oceanic and Atmospheric Administration is created and it goes on to conduct some of the most important research into climate change, including the launch of the first Landsat satellite in 1972. These satellites – there have been seven in total (although one failed to reach orbit) – have produced some of the most important images of the Earth from space, including those of shrinking ice caps.

1975 A number of different scientific reports throughout the decade start to link various gases and pollutants – methane, aerosols, ozone, CFCs, etc. – to climate change. These findings coincide with an ever-increasing environmental awareness among the public.

1977 **The National Academy of Sciences in America**, a highly respected organization, publishes a major report warning that global temperatures might rise to 'catastrophic levels' during the next couple of centuries. Media reports now openly start to talk about the role of humans in climate change.

1981 **James Hansen**, an American scientist working at NASA's Goddard Institute for Space Studies (who has since become one of the world's leading voices arguing for urgent action to cut greenhouse-gas emissions), warns that carbon dioxide in the atmosphere could lead to global warming sooner than previously predicted – as early as the year 2000. Other scientists had made similar claims before but Hansen is determined to be heard.

1987 The **Montreal Protocol** – or, to use its long name, the Montreal Protocol on Substances that Deplete the Ozone Layer – is signed by dozens of countries around the world. After scientists notice that CFCs are creating a huge hole in the ozone layer above Antarctica, the protocol ensures that CFCs are banned from use in many household items such as fridges. Within just a few years, it seems to have the desired effect and it is hailed as a good example of how politicians and scientists can unite to tackle an environmental problem.

1988 **James Hansen** tells senior US politicians at the US Senate Committee on Energy and Natural Resources that he is '99 per cent certain' that the 20th century's warming trend is not a natural variation but is being caused by a build-up of carbon dioxide and other man-made gases in the atmosphere. 'It is time to stop waffling so much and say that the evidence is pretty strong that the Greenhouse Effect is here,' he says. Al Gore, the future vice-president of the United States and maker of *An Inconvenient Truth*, is listening in the audience (see page 222).

Margaret Thatcher, Britain's prime minister, makes a speech describing global warming as a key issue of our time and orders extra research to be conducted. She is the first leading politician to say such a thing.

1990 The first report published by the **IPCC** says that climate change will cause temperatures to rise between 1.5 and 4.5°C by the middle of the 21st century.

1992 The first **'Earth Summit'** is held in Rio de Janeiro in Brazil. Many countries argue that limits are now required on the amount of greenhouse gases each country can produce.

1995 First reports of massive ice floes breaking off from Antarctica and drifting into the ocean coincide with the widespread heatwaves during what turns out to be the warmest year on record.

1997 More than 100 countries sign up to the **Kyoto Protocol**, which states that by 2008–12 these countries must have reduced their greenhouse-gas emissions by 5 per cent below their 1990 levels. The protocol is based on a 'cap and trade' system, which means that a limit is introduced on emissions, but if a country manages to emit fewer greenhouse gases than this it can then sell its 'spare quota' to a country that wishes to emit **more** than its limit.

1998 One of the largest **El Niño** seasons on record causes weather disruption all over the world, including soaring summer heatwaves across Europe. Widespread public discussion follows about our changing climate.

WILL JELLYFISH RULE THE WORLD?

2001 The third **IPCC report** says that there is 'new and stronger evidence' that most of the warming observed over the past 50 years is due to human activities. The report predicts that the average global temperature will increase by 1.4–5.8°C over the next century, and that sea levels could rise by 0.1–0.9 metres over the same period.

2003 A deadly **heatwave** in Europe kills thousands of people and leads to a large shift in public opinion about climate change, with many now believing humans are indeed responsible.

2005 Hurricane Katrina devastates New Orleans in the USA. Again, there is widespread discussion across the world about how we need to urgently tackle climate change. The Kyoto Protocol officially comes into force.

2006 Al Gore releases **An Inconvenient Truth**, a documentary about the science of climate change that goes on to win an Oscar and help earn Gore (in partnership with the IPCC) the Nobel Peace Prize. Climate change has by now become the issue of our age, with political and business leaders all over the world agreeing that something must be done. Agreeing on what needs to be done proves to be a great deal harder.

2008 Sea ice in the Arctic Circle continues to retreat at alarming levels, according to scientists. Some predict that there could be no summer ice at all within a decade. Polar bears are forced to swim many miles in open water to find ice from which to hunt for seals, leaving them exhausted and hungry.

Index

Puffin Books

Why should your eyes have all the fun?

Give your ears a treat and hear your favourite classics come to life!

Go to the Puffin Podcast
on the all-new
puffin.co.uk now!

Celebrity podcasters include Eoin Colfer, Meg Rosoff, Darren Shan and Garth Nix.

Hear Captain Hook in action, *listen* to Long John Silver, enjoy the *sound* of the Psammead and much, much more!

puffin.co.uk

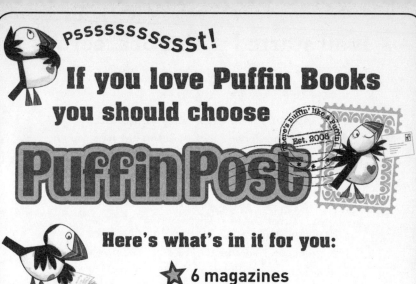

It all started with a Scarecrow

Puffin is well over sixty years old.
Sounds ancient, doesn't it? But Puffin has never been
so lively. We're always on the lookout for the next big
idea, which is how it began all those years ago.

Penguin Books was a big idea from the mind of
a man called Allen Lane, who in 1935 invented
the quality paperback and changed the world.
**And from great Penguins, great Puffins grew,
changing the face of children's books forever.**

The first four Puffin Picture Books were hatched in 1940 and the
first Puffin story book featured a man with broomstick arms called
Worzel Gummidge. In 1967 Kaye Webb, Puffin Editor, started the
Puffin Club, promising to **'make children into readers'**.
She kept that promise and over 200,000 children became
devoted Puffineers through their quarterly installments of
Puffin Post, which is now back for a new generation.

Many years from now, we hope you'll look back and
remember Puffin with a smile. **No matter what your age
or what you're into, there's a Puffin for everyone.**
The possibilities are endless, but one thing is for sure:
whether it's a picture book or a paperback, a sticker book
or a hardback, **if it's got that little Puffin
on it – it's bound to be good.**